# Junior Science
## Book 1

**GALORE PARK**

# Junior Science

# Book 1

## Sue Hunter and Jenny Macdonald

### Editor: David Penter
#### Series Editor: Louise Martine

www.galorepark.co.uk

Published by Galore Park Publishing Ltd
19/21 Sayers Lane, Tenterden, Kent TN30 6BW
www.galorepark.co.uk

Layout by Typetechnique
Technical illustrations by Ian Moores
Cartoon illustrations by Rowan Barnes-Murphy

Printed by Replika Press, India

ISBN-13: 978 1905735 17 4

First published 2008, reprinted 2010, 2011, 2012, 2013

To accompany this course:
Junior Science Teacher's Resource
(available for download from www.galorepark.co.uk
or as a CD ISBN: 978 1905735 38 9)

Details of other Galore Park publications are available at
www.galorepark.co.uk

ISEB Revision Guides, publications and examination papers may also be
obtained from Galore Park.

The following photographs are used permission of the photo libraries as indicated.
All other images are copyright © Sue Hunter.

Page 9 (L) John Reader/Science Photo Library; (R) Anthony Mercieca/Science Photo Library;
page 10 (TL) Gustoimages/Science Photo Library; (BL) Martin Bond/Science Photo Library;
(R) Aflo Co UK/Alamy; page 11 (T) Maximilian Stock Ltd/Science Photo Library; (B) David
Munns/Science Photo Library; page 13 (T) Leonard Rue Enterprises/Science Photo Library;
(B) Dr P Marazzi/Science Photo Library; page 14 (T) Gregory G Dimijian, MD/Photo
Researchers, Inc; (BL) Daniel Sambraus / Science Photo Library; (BC) Neal Grundy/Science
Photo Library; (BR) D. Roberts/Science Photo Library; page 17 Michael Donne/Science
Photo Library; page 29 Simon Booth/Science Photo Library; page 30 (T) Andy
Harmer/Science Photo Library; (TL) Barbara Strnadova/Science Photo Library; (BR)
David Aubrey/Science Photo Library; page 41 Simon Fraser/Science Photo Library; page 42
Gustoimages/Science Photo Library; page 46 Sajjad Hussain/AFP/Getty Images; page 47 (T)
Stephen & Donna O'Meara/Science Photo Library; page 57 (T) Sinclair Stammers/Science
Photo Library; (B) John Elk III/Alamy; page 60 David R. Frazier/Science Photo Library; page
61 Kokoro/NHMPL; page 75 (T) View Stock/Alamy; (B) National Maritime Museum,
Greenwich, London, Gabb Collection; page 85 Hans-Ulrich Osterwalder/Science Photo
Library; page 86 (T) Andrew Syred/Science Photo Library; (C) Susumu Nishinaga/Science
Photo Library; (B) Cordelia Molloy / Science Photo Library; page 97 Martin Bond/Science
Photo Library; page 109 Jim Amos/ Science Photo Library; page 110 David Hancock/Alamy;
page 112 Scott Camazine/Science Photo Library; page 113 (TL) Dr Keith Wheeler/Science
Photo Library;(BR) Dr Jeremy Burgess/Science Photo Library

# About the authors

Sue Hunter has been a science teacher in a variety of schools for more years than she cares to remember. Her experiences have included teaching in a choir school and a London middle school, teaching GSCE and A level in the Netherlands and a short spell as a full-time mother of two. She is Head of Science at St Hugh's School in Oxfordshire and a member of the Common Entrance 11+ setting team. She has run a number of training courses for prep school teachers, including at Malvern College and for the Independent Association of Prep Schools (IAPS), and is currently IAPS Support Co-ordinator for science and a member of the Independent Schools Inspectorate.

Jenny Macdonald has been a teacher since graduating in 1973, teaching in both state and private schools, and for the last ten years has taught science to Years 3 to 6 at St Hugh's School in Oxfordshire. After marrying in the mid-1970s, she moved to Oxfordshire and in the 1980s the family acquired a smallholding where she raised three children before graduating to sheep, chickens, cats and dogs. She is a keen singer in several local choirs, enjoys outdoor pursuits and has travelled extensively, helping her husband undertake research work on wildlife conservation projects around the world.

# Note to teachers

The Teacher's Resource (available as a download or on CD) which accompanies this title, contains valuable worksheets for the 'To do' exercises including a useful note on resources, lists of key vocabulary and topic summaries with learning objectives.

# Preface

*The most exciting phrase to hear in science, the one that heralds new discoveries, is not 'Eureka!' but 'That's funny ...'* **Isaac Asimov**

The study of science for young children is a voyage of discovery. It stimulates their curiosity and provides a vehicle for them to explore their world, to ask questions about things that they observe and to make sense of their observations. It does not exist in isolation but draws upon many other aspects of a well-rounded curriculum and should be practical, interesting and, above all, fun.

This book is the first of three Junior Science books designed to be used in Years 3 to 5. The three books together can be used to underpin a course of study leading to the 11+ Common Entrance examinations and link directly into *So You Really Want to Learn Science* Books 1 and 2, by Ron Pickering. The books are designed in such a way that they can be used as a course in their own right, one book for each of Years 3 to 5, or as a resource to support an existing scheme of work.

# Acknowledgements

We are immensely grateful to Louise Martine, Terry Hardy and Kay Macmullan for their support in preparing this book and to David Penter for casting his expert eye over the script.

Thanks must also go to our families for putting up with erratically-timed meals, producing cups of coffee and tea or glasses of wine at appropriate moments and providing support and encouragement throughout the gestation period of the book.

Lastly, we should thank the pupils at St Hugh's School, Carswell, for (unwittingly) acting as guinea pigs for much of the material in the book. Their unfailing enthusiasm for science has been our inspiration and this book is for them.

Sue Hunter and Jenny Macdonald
September 2008

# Contents

## Introduction

## Chapter 1: Our bodies

## Chapter 2: Vertebrates and invertebrates

## Chapter 3: Rocks

## Chapter 4: Magnets

# Chapter 5: Light and shadows

# Chapter 6: Materials

# Index

# Introduction

## What is science?

The word 'science' comes from the Latin word for knowledge, so science is knowledge. However, we generally think of science as being the study of the world around us.

Through scientific discovery, we can find out about the huge number of different types of plants and animals that live in our world, on the planet Earth. We can find out about where they live, how they feed and breed and how they all depend on each other. It is very useful to understand how our actions affect the other living things that share the Earth with us. Understanding about us as humans is interesting because we can learn about how our bodies work and what we can do to keep ourselves fit and healthy.

There are lots of different things to study in our world. We can find out about the structure of the Earth and the rocks and soils that form its surface. From these rocks we can obtain chemicals and materials to use in our everyday lives. We need to find out about these materials, how they behave and how they can be used to make the things we need. This knowledge can then be used to help us produce new materials or make better use of the ones we already have.

It is very exciting to investigate and look carefully at the way things work, the forces that make things move and the energy that drives them all. We can look up and study the planets, stars and galaxies that make up the Universe. New discoveries are being made all the time and there is still a lot that we don't know about the Universe and the way it works.

When you study science at school, you will learn about things that other people have discovered. But anyone can find out something new that no one has ever thought of before. The important thing is to take an interest in everything that is going on around you, to think about what you see and hear and to ask questions about anything that puzzles you. The world is a huge and complicated place. We don't know everything about it so there is always something worth investigating. All you have to do is to find it. And, who knows – you might discover something new!

Studying the world around us

## To do: What do scientists do?

There are many different types of scientist who study many different things. They are often given special names, which give us a clue to the sort of things they investigate. See if you can find out what would be studied by each of the following kinds of scientist:

astronomer                          geologist
biologist                           herpetologist
botanist                            palaeontologist
entomologist                        physicist

# How to be a scientist

Scientists find out about the world around them in a number of ways. To be a good scientist you need to:

- Observe
- Record
- Ask questions
- Find answers
- Work safely

## Observe

Good scientists are always observing

As you go about your daily lives, you take in lots of information about the world around you. Your five senses (sight, hearing, smell, taste and touch) are busy all the time. When you notice something interesting, you can look more closely or listen more carefully to find out more. This is observing and good scientists do it all the time.

## Record

Keeping records is an important part of being a scientist

Scientists keep records of their observations. Records could be notes, photographs, diagrams, measurements or video or sound recordings. Recording the things they have observed helps them to remember the interesting facts they have discovered. They can use their records to help them to find patterns in their observations so that they can explain what they observe.

## Ask questions

Asking questions helps you to learn

Observation often leads to questions. Questions lead you to investigate further. Asking questions is one of the best ways of learning more about the world around you. Often your parents or teachers can answer your questions. Sometimes they cannot so you will need to find out for yourself.

## Find answers

Research may give you the answers to your questions

There are many ways to find answers to your questions. You can observe more closely or look in books or on the internet. Most scientists will find the answers to their questions by doing experiments. You will be doing lots of experiments during your study of science. To be a successful experimenter, you need to work sensibly and safely. You need to observe carefully and measure accurately. You need to record your results clearly. Most importantly, you need to think about what you find and see what your results tell you.

You may not realise it, but you have been a scientist all your life. Even very small babies observe the world around them and young children ask questions all the time. Your science lessons will help you to become an even better scientist.

## Work safely

You may have your science lessons in your classroom or you may go to a special science room, called a laboratory. Wherever you are studying, it is very important that you work safely at all times, especially when doing experiments. Your school will have a special set of rules that you must follow when doing science experiments and it is important to remember them. Good scientists are always thinking about whether they are working safely.

### To do: Safety first

Look at this picture. Some of the children are working safely and some are not. With your partner or group, decide which children are acting safely and why. Then find the children who are not acting safely and say what they should do differently.

Here are some basic rules for working safely in science. For each rule, explain why it is important and what could happen if you did not obey it.

1. Always listen to instructions and follow them carefully.

2. Do not play around with science equipment. Always use it carefully and sensibly.

3. Never run around when doing science experiments.

4. If you are given goggles or safety glasses to wear, keep them on until you are told that it is safe to remove them.

5. Keep all substances and equipment away from your mouth.

## A fair test

When we are trying to find answers to our questions, we often need to do experiments to test our ideas. When we do this we must make sure that our tests are fair. This means that we must try to keep everything exactly the same each time, apart from the one thing that we are testing (see page 103).

# Chapter 1: Our bodies

The human body is the cleverest and most complicated machine ever built! It is made up of millions and millions of tiny living parts called cells. Each cell is specially made to do a particular job. The 'human body machine' repairs itself when it is damaged. Its control centre, the brain, keeps it all working properly and guides it to do all sorts of different things. It is truly amazing. You need to look after your own 'human body machine'. To help you to do this, you need to learn more about what it contains and how it works.

## What is inside?

The cells that make up our bodies are grouped together to make the working parts, called **organs**. Some of the important organs that we will be learning about are shown on this diagram.

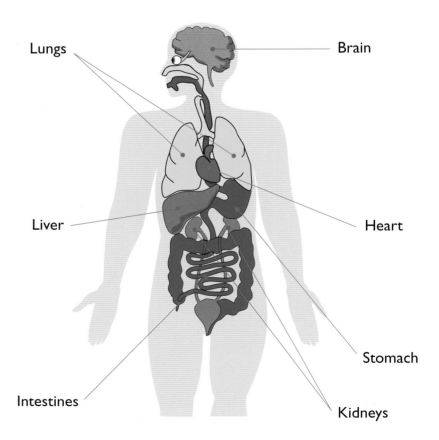

Organs inside the body

Each of these organs has a special job to do.

The **brain** is the control centre for our bodies.

The **heart** pumps the blood around the body, carrying important substances such as **oxygen** and dissolved food to our cells and waste products away from them.

The **lungs** take in oxygen from the air and get rid of carbon dioxide from our bodies.

The **stomach** digests our food so that it can be used in our bodies.

The **intestines** take the digested food into the blood so that it can be carried to the cells.

The **liver** has many jobs, including cleaning some poisonous substances such as alcohol out of our blood.

The **kidneys** clear poisons and excess water out of the blood.

There are many other organs in our bodies and you will learn more about them later.

All these important organs are safely held inside an outer layer of flexible, waterproof skin, and the whole body is supported and protected by a strong skeleton (see page 20).

**Did you know?**
The brain sends messages to the rest of the body by sending tiny electrical signals down a 'wiring system' of **nerves**.

**Did you know?**
An adult's intestines are about 10 metres long. They are carefully looped up to fit into the body.

**Did you know?**
Cells were first named by Robert Hooke in his book, *Micrographia*, in 1665. When looking at a thin slice of cork through his **microscope**, he saw that it was divided into tiny sections. He thought they looked like the small rooms called cells where monks slept.

## To do: Just a minute

Find out how many times your heart beats in one minute. You will need to find a place on your neck or wrist where you can feel the regular pumping of blood through an artery. This is called a **pulse** point. When you have found it, count the beats you can feel in one minute.

You can feel your pulse on your neck

# Exercise 1.1

Fill the gaps in these sentences, using the following words:

> carbon dioxide    stomach    heart    oxygen    organs
> oxygen    cells    nutrients

1.    The working parts inside the body are called _____.

2.    These are made up of millions of _____.

3.    The lungs bring _____ into the body and send _____ out of the body.

4.    The _____ is where our food is digested.

5.    The _____ pumps blood around the body to carry _____ and _____ to the cells.

· · · · · · · · · · · · · · · · · · · · · · · · · · · · · · · · · · · · · · · · · · · · · · ·

# Exercise 1.2

1.    Which organ sends electrical messages to control your body?

2.    Where in your body is your food digested?

3. Name two important things that are carried around the body in your blood.

4. What is the function (job) of the heart?

5. What is a pulse point?

. . . . . . . . . . . . . . . . . . . . . . . . . . . . . . . . . . . . . . . . . . . .

# Exercise 1.3: Extension question

When you found out how many times your heart beats in a minute, you probably found that other members of the class recorded different results. Can you think of any reasons why this might be?

. . . . . . . . . . . . . . . . . . . . . . . . . . . . . . . . . . . . . . . . . . . .

# Fuel for our bodies

Like any machine, our bodies need fuel to keep them working properly. This fuel comes from the food we eat and so our **diet** has to contain foods that provide us with all the **energy** we need. It must also contain the **materials** the body needs to build new cells for growth and repair and the substances needed to keep the whole system working healthily.

## Our diet

The word diet is often used to refer to losing weight. Its real meaning is the range of food and drink that we take into our bodies. Animals have diets too. Their diets are often very different to ours.

Lions and hummingbirds have very different diets

We need to choose the foods we eat carefully. Foods contain special substances called **nutrients**. Different foods contain different nutrients. We should choose a range of different foods to make sure that we are eating all the important nutrients that our bodies need.

## Nutrients for energy

To provide us with energy we should eat foods containing two types of nutrients: **carbohydrates** and **fats**.

Starchy foods

### Carbohydrates

There are two kinds of carbohydrate: **starch** and **sugars**. Starchy foods are those such as bread, rice, pasta, potatoes and cereals. These foods provide a good source of energy to see us through the day.

Sugars are found in sweets, cakes and ice cream, and in fruit. They release their energy quickly. We should try not to eat too many sugary foods because they cause tooth decay (see page 16).

Sweet foods

Fats are found in various different foods

### Fats

Fats are found in meat, fish, dairy products (milk, butter, cheese and yoghurt) and also in foods such as burgers, chips and crisps.

It is important to have fat in our diet. We store fat under our skin and it helps us to stay warm as well as being a useful source of energy. Too much fat can make us **obese** (overweight) and can also cause heart disease, so we must limit the amount of fat that we eat.

## Nutrients for growth and repair

The body needs materials to build new cells. These materials come from nutrients called **proteins**.

Proteins are found in meat, fish and eggs. Some people, such as vegetarians, do not eat these foods. We can also get proteins from dairy products and from nuts and pulses (beans and lentils).

Foods containing protein

## Nutrients for health

**Vitamins** and **minerals** help to keep our bodies healthy and working properly. To get enough of these, we need to eat a wide variety of different foods, especially dairy products, fruit and vegetables. (See page 23 to learn more about vitamins.)

## A balanced diet

By using a **food pyramid**, we can check that the balance of our diet is right and that we are providing our bodies with all the nutrients we need. We also need to make sure that our food has plenty of fibre, and that we drink lots too.

A food pyramid is divided up into sections. The larger sections at the bottom contain those foods that we should eat most of. The smaller sections show those foods that we should not eat so often.

**To do: Food pyramids**

1. Make your own food pyramid, illustrating it with pictures of your favourite foods.

2. Write the names of some foods on small cards or slips of paper. Time yourself to see how quickly you can sort them into the right places on the food pyramid. Challenge your friends to a race.

3. Design a perfectly balanced sandwich. Think about which type of bread you might use, what you might spread on the bread and any other foods you might include to make it both delicious and healthy. Try to include foods from each section of the food pyramid.

# Exercise 1.4

Fill the gaps in these sentences, using the following words:

| | | | | | |
|---|---|---|---|---|---|
| starchy | obesity | fruit | energy | sugary | nutrients |
| warm | diet | carbohydrates | grow | potatoes | |

1. We should try to eat a balanced _____ in order to provide our bodies with all the _____ that they need.

2. _____ provide us with energy and can be found in _____ foods, such as bread and _____ or in _____ foods, such as biscuits and _____.

3. Fat is needed as a store of _____ and to keep us _____.

4. Too much fat causes _____ and heart disease.

5. We need protein to help us to _____.

# Exercise 1.5

1. Name two types of nutrients that we can eat to give us energy.

2. Explain why we need to eat foods containing proteins.

3. Give two reasons why it is important to eat some foods containing fat.

4. Give two reasons why it is important not to eat too much fat.

5. We are often told to eat five helpings of fruits and vegetables each day. Explain why these foods are necessary.

· · · · · · · · · · · · · · · · · · · · · · · · · · · · · · · · · · · · · · ·

## Exercise 1.6: Extension question

A dietician is someone who advises people about what they should be eating to remain healthy. Imagine that you are a dietician and write a letter to one of your patients, explaining how to use a food pyramid to help choose a healthy, balanced diet.

· · · · · · · · · · · · · · · · · · · · · · · · · · · · · · · · · · · · · · ·

## Teeth

There are many different types of tooth. Different animals have different teeth and these teeth are specially designed to help the animal to obtain its food.

There are four main types of tooth: incisors, canines, premolars and molars.

**Incisors** are broad, thin teeth shaped like a knife blade. They are useful for biting and cutting through food such as grass but are also useful for gnawing away at tougher materials such as wood.

Beavers have large incisors

**Canines** are sharp, pointed teeth. They are useful for tearing meat and catching hold of moving prey.

Lions have sharp canines

**Premolars** and **molars** are broad teeth with a ridged or bumpy surface. They are used for grinding or chewing food. Some molars are very big indeed.

Elephants' teeth are huge and have tough grinding surfaces

## To do: Animal teeth

We can tell a lot about an animal's diet by looking at its teeth. Look at these skulls and the differences between the teeth. Can you explain how each animal's teeth help it to obtain its food?

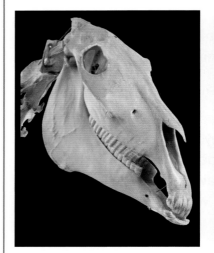

A horse skull

A tiger skull

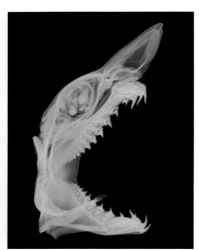

A shark skull

## Human teeth

Because humans eat a wide variety of different foods, we have all four different types of teeth. Incisors at the front of the mouth cut our food into pieces small enough to fit into our mouths. Sharper canines help to tear at tougher foods. At the back of the mouth, we have premolars and molars to chew the food to make it soft enough to swallow.

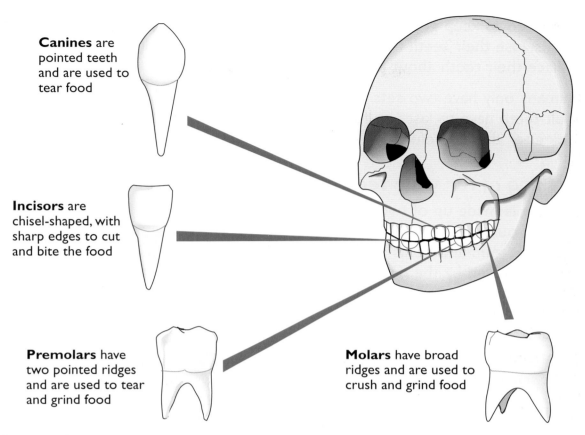

**Canines** are pointed teeth and are used to tear food

**Incisors** are chisel-shaped, with sharp edges to cut and bite the food

**Premolars** have two pointed ridges and are used to tear and grind food

**Molars** have broad ridges and are used to crush and grind food

Human teeth

Human babies are born without teeth. When they are about five or six months old, their first teeth begin to show through the gums. These are part of their first set of teeth, often called 'milk teeth'. It usually takes about three years for all the teeth to come through.

Because a baby's jaws are not very big, there are only 20 milk teeth. When the child is a bit older, usually about five or six years old, these first teeth begin to fall out and are replaced by new, adult teeth. When all these teeth have come through, there will be 32 of them.

Some animals, such as elephants, have teeth that continue growing all through their lives. The rough plant material that elephants eat wears away the teeth so

When a shark's working tooth is lost, it is replaced by the tooth behind it

they need to keep growing or the animal will starve. Some animals, such as sharks, lose their teeth frequently and grow new ones. Some sharks will replace their teeth about every two weeks.

Humans only have two sets of teeth, the milk teeth and the adult ones. Your adult teeth have to last you for the rest of your life so it is important to look after them carefully.

## Looking after your teeth

A tooth is made up of two parts: the crown and the root. The part that you can see, outside the gum, is called the **crown**. The other part, which sits inside the gum and holds it in place, is called the **root**. Unless you have a tooth removed by the dentist, you will never see the roots of your teeth. When your milk teeth fall out, the root has been dissolved away so you only see the crown.

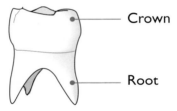

Crown

Root

A molar, showing the crown and the root

If you look inside a tooth, you can see that it is made up of three layers. The outside layer of the crown is the hard, shiny surface called the **enamel**. Inside the enamel is a softer layer called **dentine** and in the middle is an area that contains blood vessels and nerves. This is called the **pulp**.

To keep your teeth healthy you need to make sure that the hard enamel layer is not damaged. Sometimes, teeth are damaged by an accident, but most damage is caused by tiny living things called **bacteria** that live in the mouth. They form a layer on the teeth, called **plaque**.

Bacteria feed on sugar and so when you put sugary foods or drinks in your mouth, the bacteria begin to feed on the sugars. As they do so, they turn the sugar into acid. If it is not cleaned off, the acid can eat away the enamel surface of the tooth, making a tiny hole called a **cavity**.

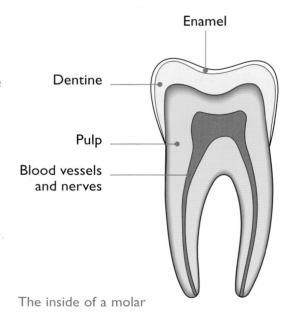

Enamel

Dentine

Pulp

Blood vessels and nerves

The inside of a molar

This cavity is a good place for bacteria to live because you cannot brush them away easily. They continue to feed on sugars, making more acid and the cavity gets bigger and bigger. If the dentist does not find the hole and mend it, the acid will wear away the soft dentine, right through to the pulp where the nerves are. Ouch!

To prevent this happening, you need to try to keep the bacteria away and make sure that they are not too well fed.

The most important thing is to make sure that your teeth are properly cleaned at least twice a day using a good brush and toothpaste. You should scrub your teeth gently but thoroughly for about two minutes. This seems like a very long time but it is the best way to remove all the plaque. It is a good idea to include your gums in the brushing as well to make sure that all the bacteria are cleaned off.

Many people clean between their teeth using dental floss to make sure that the bacteria are cleaned way from these places as well. To check that you are cleaning your teeth properly, you might use a disclosing tablet.

Bacteria make acid from sugar so it is best to make sure that you do not eat too many sugary foods. Sweet fizzy drinks are really bad for your teeth because they contain acid as well as sugar.

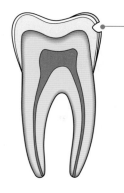

A cavity caused by acid eating away the enamel surface

A hole in the enamel of a tooth is called a cavity

Acid eats through dentine to pulp

If a cavity is not filled, it will get bigger

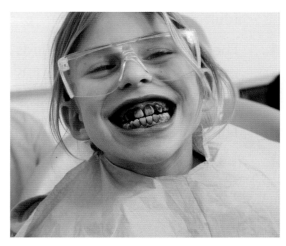

Using a disclosing tablet. The pink stains show where the plaque needs to be brushed away

You should visit your **dentist** regularly, about twice a year. The dentist will check your teeth and can clean out and fill any cavities that have formed before they get too big.

Regular visits to the dentist are important

## To do: Smile please

Design a leaflet or poster reminding children about how to keep their teeth healthy.

# Exercise 1.7

Fill the gaps in these sentences, using the following words:

bacteria    cavities    molars    milk    canines    enamel
adult    incisors    acid    premolars

1.  There are four different kinds of teeth. They are called _____, _____, _____, and _____.

2.  When children are about five, their _____ teeth begin to fall out.

3.  These are then replaced by _____ teeth.

4.  If we do not clean our teeth, _____ will turn sugar into _____ which will damage the _____ and make _____.

# Exercise 1.8

1. Name the four main types of teeth.

2. Describe the function of each type of tooth.

3. What is the name of the part of the tooth that can be seen outside the gum?

4. What is enamel?

5. How many milk teeth do children have?

6. How many teeth do adults have?

7. What is the name given to the layer of bacteria that builds up on our teeth?

8. Explain in your own words how bacteria cause the teeth to decay.

9. What three things can you do to make sure that your teeth stay healthy?

# Exercise 1.9: Extension questions

1. Suggest a reason why human babies are born without teeth.

2. Imagine that you are a bacterium on the teeth of a young child. Write a diary entry for a day. Include details about what the child eats and what happens when the child cleans his or her teeth and visits the dentist.

# Bones and joints

**Bones** are hard and strong. Together, they make a kind of scaffolding inside our bodies.

We call this scaffolding a **skeleton**. Our skeleton has three main functions:

1. It **supports** the body, keeping it upright and in the right shape.

2. It **protects** the most important organs in the body.

3. It makes a strong structure for the muscles to pull on so we can **move** our bodies.

## Support

Here is a diagram of a human skeleton. You can see how all the bones fit together to support the body.

**Did you know?**
Babies are born with about 300 bones but some of them join together and adults have only 206 bones.

## Protection

One of the functions of the skeleton is to protect the most important organs – the heart, lungs and brain. The brain is protected inside the skull and the rib cage protects the heart and lungs.

## Movement

Our bones move when the muscles pull on them. The movement takes place at the joints between the bones. A **joint** is where two or more bones meet. We have lots of joints so our bodies can be flexible. Imagine what it would be like without so many joints. If you had no elbow joints, could you pick up a pencil from the table in front of you and write in your book? How would you eat? Could you ride a bicycle without knee joints? What sports would be possible without elbows or knees?

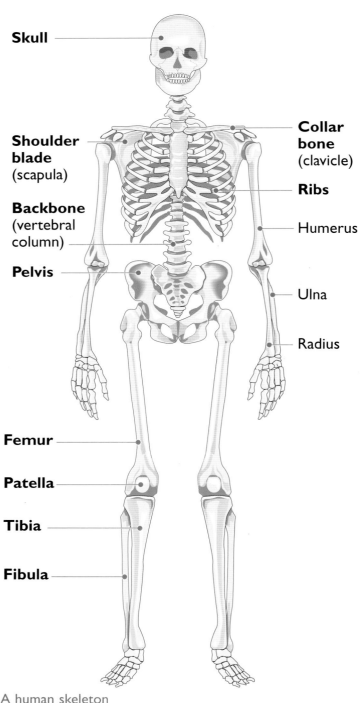

Skull

Collar bone (clavicle)

Shoulder blade (scapula)

Ribs

Backbone (vertebral column)

Humerus

Pelvis

Ulna

Radius

Femur

Patella

Tibia

Fibula

A human skeleton

## How do joints work?

Joints are moved by **muscles**. Muscles can only do two things: they can **contract**, which means they get shorter, and then **relax** back to their original length. They cannot stretch. When we move a joint we need at least two muscles to pull the joint in different directions.

The **elbow joint** is closed and opened by two muscles.

Without joints, it would be very difficult to move

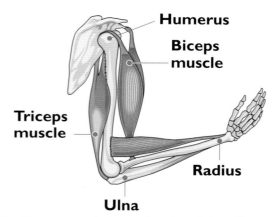

The biceps muscle is used to bend the elbow

To close the elbow joint, the biceps muscle contracts (gets shorter). One end of the muscle is attached to the upper arm bone (humerus) and the other end is attached to the lower arm bone (radius). When the muscle contracts it pulls these two bones together as if it were closing a door.

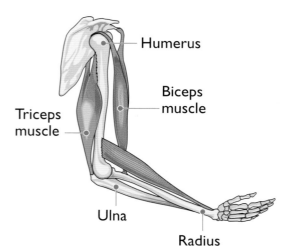

The triceps muscle is used to straighten the elbow

To open the joint again, the biceps muscle relaxes while the triceps muscle contracts. This pulls the bones in the opposite direction.

This type of joint is called a **hinge joint** because it opens and closes like the hinge on a door.

Our hip joints can move in several different directions, a bit like a joystick control for a computer game. This type of joint is called a **ball and socket joint**.

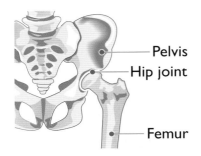

Pelvis

Hip joint

Femur

A hip joint is a ball and socket joint

**Did you know?**
Muscles can pull on skin as well as bones. It takes 43 muscles to frown but only 17 to smile.

# Exercise 1.10

Fill the gaps in these sentences, using the following words:

| contracts | heart | two | lungs | relaxes | joints | skeleton |
|---|---|---|---|---|---|---|

1. The bones in our bodies are joined together to make a
   _____.

2. The _____ and _____ are protected by the rib cage.

3. Places where two or more bones come together are called
   _____.

4. _____ muscles are needed in order to move a joint – one _____, or gets shorter, while the other _____.

# Exercise 1.11

1. What are the three main functions of the skeleton?

2. Which important organ is found inside the skull?

3. What is a joint?

4. Why do we have so many joints in our bodies?

5. Which two muscles work together to move the elbow joint?

6. Two types of joint are mentioned in this chapter: hinge joints and ball and socket joints. Which type of joint is each of the following?

   (a) elbow

   (b) hip

   (c) shoulder

   (d) knee

## Exercise 1.12: Extension questions

1. Look at the picture of a skeleton on page 20.

   (a) Which bones in the human body do you think are the strongest?

   (b) Suggest reasons why these bones are stronger than the others.

2. Imagine that you have no elbow or knee joints. Which everyday activities would you find hard? What could you do to make these activities easier?

## The story of scurvy

Scurvy is a disease caused by lack of vitamin C in the diet. People knew about the disease as long ago as the 4th century BC but it was not properly investigated until people started making long sea voyages in the 15th century. On some of these long voyages as many as three-quarters of the people on the ship died from the disease. No one knew then what caused it so they did not know what to do to stay healthy. As the sickness usually began after 12 weeks at sea, one theory was that it was bad air over the sea that made them ill.

When the Portuguese explorer Vasco da Gama sailed from Lisbon to try to find a route to the Spice Islands, in Indonesia, many of his sailors fell ill with scurvy. Sailors with scurvy found that their gums became sore, their teeth began to fall out and their skin became black. Some of da Gama's men died and others were close to death when they were rescued by a ship from Mombassa on the coast of Kenya. This ship was carrying a load of oranges and the sick men sucked them hungrily because they were unable to eat properly. All the men recovered quickly from the disease.

In around 1700, a new method of preserving oranges was developed. It was based on a Portuguese sweet, made from quinces, called *marmelada*. The first marmalade as we know it now was probably made in Scotland. Marmalade was taken on board many ships and the vitamin C that it provided kept many sailors from developing scurvy.

In 1753, James Lind, a ship's doctor, published a book called *A Treatise on the Scurvy*. He had proved that citrus fruit could be used to prevent and cure this terrible disease. He thought that any acidic food would do if fruit was not available. Ships started to carry stores of foods such as sauerkraut (pickled cabbage), malt and dried vegetable soup to try to cure sailors who developed scurvy. In fact, none of these foods contain the vitamin C that is needed to prevent scurvy but they probably helped the crew to remain healthy in other ways.

Sailors with scurvy lost their teeth and their skin turned black

Between 1769 and 1771, Captain James Cook sailed from Britain, half way round the world to discover Australia. He took great care over the health of his crew. When he returned to Britain in 1771, it was reported that not one member of his crew had died from scurvy. This was the first time that a long voyage had ended without any deaths from the disease.

It was not until 1932 that scientists finally showed that vitamin C was needed in the diet to prevent scurvy. Refrigerators made it possible to keep fresh foods on board ship so sailors could be provided with fresh citrus fruits to keep them healthy. People can still develop scurvy if they do not eat enough foods containing vitamin C so this is a good reason to include plenty of oranges and other fruit in your diet.

## Exercise 1.13

Fill in the gaps in these sentences using the words in the box below.

> Australia   12   marmalade   black   vitamin C
> teeth   air   oranges

1. People can suffer from scurvy if they do not eat enough _____.

2. Sailors often developed scurvy after about _____ weeks at sea. They thought it was caused by bad _____.

3. People with scurvy lose their _____ and their skin becomes _____.

4. Sailors in Vasco da Gama's ship were cured by sucking _____.

5. Some ships began to carry oranges made into _____ to help the sailors stay healthy.

6. The first long sea voyage on which no one died from scurvy was when Captain Cook sailed to discover _____ .

# Exercise 1.14

1. Which nutrient is needed in the diet to prevent scurvy?

2. What did people in the 15th century believe was the cause of scurvy?

3. What are the symptoms (effects on the body) of scurvy?

4. Where did Vasco da Gama sail from when he tried to find a route to the Spice Islands?

5. How were his sailors cured of scurvy?

6. What was the name of the ship's doctor who investigated the causes of scurvy in the 18th century?

7. What fruit was used to make the Portugese sweet called marmelada?

8. Apart from the discovery of Australia, what was special about Captain Cook's voyage in 1769–1771?

# Exercise 1.15: Extension question

Sailors on modern ships do not often suffer from diseases caused by poor diet. Suggest why this might be. Try to think of as many reasons as possible.

# Chapter 2: Vertebrates and invertebrates

## Sorting living things

No one knows how many different types of **organisms** (living things) there are on Earth. We know about millions but there may be millions more still to find.

In order to understand plants and animals and how they live and adapt to their different habitats (areas in which they live), we need to divide them into groups, putting together organisms that are similar to each other in some way.

The easiest way to do this is to ask a simple question to which the answer will be either YES or NO, and make something called a **branching key**.

One of the first questions we can ask about all living things is:

### Can it make its own food from water and carbon dioxide?

**NO**
It is an **animal**.

**YES**
It is a **plant**.

In this chapter, we are going to think about different types of animal. The first thing to do to start an investigation, is to ask another question:

**Does it have a backbone?**

| **YES**<br>It is a vertebrate. | **NO**<br>It is an invertebrate. |
|---|---|
| 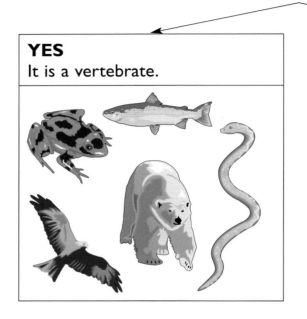 |  |

# Vertebrates

**Vertebrates** are animals with a **backbone** or spine. The backbone is made up of lots of smaller bones called **vertebrae**. This name comes from the Latin word *vertere,* which means 'to turn'. Vertebrates can bend and turn their backbone. The backbone protects important nerves that send messages from the brain to all the other parts of the body.

Most vertebrates have a bony skull to protect their brain, ribs to protect their heart, lungs and other delicate organs, and one or two pairs of limbs. In most vertebrates the skeleton is made of bone.

## Sorting vertebrates

Animals with a backbone can be divided into five further groups, by asking these questions.

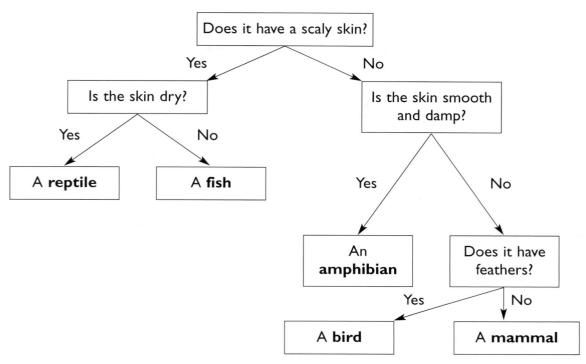

A vertebrate key

There are more than **50 000** species of vertebrates and they can all be sorted into these five groups. All the animals in each of these groups have features in common with each other.

## Fish

Examples: cod, shark, stickleback

- Fish live in water. They are **cold blooded**, which means that their body temperature is the same temperature as their surroundings.

- They can live in both fresh and salt water, except the Dead Sea where it is too salty.

- They use gills to obtain oxygen from the water.

- They have wet scales on their skin.

- They lay their eggs in water.

Male stickleback

## Amphibians

Examples: frog, newt, salamander

- Amphibians were the first animals to come out of the water onto land, over 300 million years ago.

- They are cold blooded, and usually start life in water, as tadpoles.

- Tadpoles get oxygen from the water with gills.

- When they are older, they change into the adult form. This change is called metamorphosis.

Unlike frogs and toads, newts spend most of their time in water

- Most adult amphibians live on the land, and breathe with lungs.

- In order to breed, they return to the water where they lay jelly-coated eggs.

## Reptiles

Examples: crocodile, lizard, snake, iguana

- Reptiles are cold blooded vertebrates and can often be seen sun-bathing to warm their bodies.

- Reptiles breathe with lungs.

Land iguana, Galapagos Islands

- Most reptiles lay eggs with hard or leathery shells, usually in sand. The young are fully formed when they hatch. Some snakes and lizards keep the egg inside their body and give birth to live young. A young reptile must look after itself as soon as it has been hatched.

- The skin of a reptile is dry and usually covered in scales.

- Reptiles have been on Earth for more than 300 million years.

## Birds

Examples: robin, kingfisher, ostrich

Waved albatross

- Birds are **warm blooded** vertebrates. This means that they can keep their own bodies warm.

- Birds have wings (although not all birds fly) and bodies covered with feathers to help keep them warm.

- Birds have lungs for breathing.

- The female lays eggs with hard shells, and chicks hatch from these. The young birds are cared for by the adults until they can fend for themselves.

## Mammals

Examples: rabbit, dolphin, human

Sea lion with young

- Mammals are warm blooded and most of them have hair or fur to help keep them warm. The female keeps the young inside her body until they are ready to be born. Then the mother will feed the babies with milk.

- Mammals have lungs, and can live on both land and in the water. Mammals that live in water must come to the surface to breathe.

- The largest mammal is the blue whale, which can be more than 30 m in length.

- The smallest are shrews and mice, which can be just 5 cm long (excluding their tails).

A duck-billed platypus

Sorting animals into the correct groups is not always easy. The duck-billed platypus was first discovered in Australia in 1798. Captain John Hunter sent a skin back to England so that scientists could study it but they thought that it was a hoax! Platypuses are warm blooded and have fur on their bodies like mammals but they lay eggs that are like those of a reptile. The young are fed on milk. Their feet are webbed and their leathery bill makes them look like a duck. No wonder the scientists were confused! Which group do you think they belong to?

## Exercise 2.1

Fill the gaps in these sentences, using the following words:

> reptiles  branching key  lungs    fur    mammals  gills
> milk  amphibians    backbone

1. A _____ helps us to divide organisms into groups that have similarities.

2. Vertebrates are animals that have a _____.

3. Vertebrates can be divided into five groups: fish, _____, _____, _____ and birds.

4. Fish and most young amphibians have _____ to get oxygen from the water.

5. Reptiles, birds, mammals and most adult amphibians have _____ for breathing.

6. Mammals have _____ on their bodies and feed their young with _____.

# Exercise 2.2

1. What do all vertebrates have in common?

2. Which vertebrate groups are warm blooded?

3. Describe the body coverings that these warm-blooded animals have to help them to keep warm.

4. What does the term 'cold blooded' mean?

5. Which vertebrate groups are cold blooded?

6. How do these animals warm up their bodies?

7. Which animals use lungs for breathing?

8. Which animals feed on their mothers' milk when they are young?

9. Penguins do not fly. How do they use their wings to help them get about?

# Exercise 2.3: Extension question

Reptiles and amphibians have some features that are similar and some that are different. Look at the pictures of the land iguana (reptile) on page 30 and the newt (amphibian) on page 30. Read the passages about reptiles and amphibians again. Copy the table below and then write in as many similarities and differences as you can find. Some have been done for you.

| Reptiles and amphibians | |
|---|---|
| **Similarities** | **Differences** |
| They both have four legs. | Young amphibians are tadpoles but young reptiles look like their parents. |
| | |

# Invertebrates

Animals that do not have a spine or backbone are called **invertebrates**. There are more than a million different types of invertebrates. It is not always easy to tell if an animal has a backbone, because some of them have hard protective covers and shells. Invertebrates include animals such as **insects**, **spiders**, crabs, starfish, shellfish and octopuses.

Two of the groups that have hard protective covers, called **exoskeletons**, are insects and spiders.

## Insects

Insects live all over the world, and there are more different types of insect than all the other kinds of mammals, fish, birds and reptiles put together. More than 850 000 different types of insects have been identified and people are still discovering new species. Roughly eight out of ten of all the animals on Earth are insects.

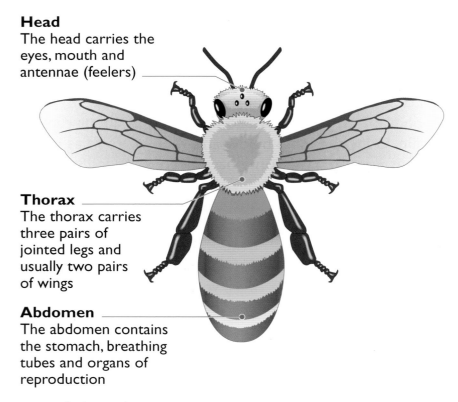

**Head**
The head carries the eyes, mouth and antennae (feelers)

**Thorax**
The thorax carries three pairs of jointed legs and usually two pairs of wings

**Abdomen**
The abdomen contains the stomach, breathing tubes and organs of reproduction

The body structure of a honey bee

Some insects are so small that they can only be seen through a microscope, others are as large as your hand. Some insects, such as bees, ants and termites, live in large groups called colonies. Some insects, such as the desert locust, can be very harmful and destroy farmers' crops. Other flying insects, such as bees, are needed to pollinate the flowers, and without them fruit trees would bear no fruit.

Insects

- have **three body parts**
- have **six legs**
- often have wings.

Mexican red-legged tarantula

## Spiders

Spiders

- have only **two body parts**
- have **eight legs**
- do not have wings or feelers
- are not insects.

All spiders spin silk threads, and many use them to trap insects so that they can eat them. Some spiders hunt and chase their prey, while others lie in wait and pounce. When a spider catches something, it will stun or kill it with a poisonous bite. All spiders have a poisonous bite, but in most cases it will not harm people.

The orb web of the garden spider is difficult to see unless it is covered with dew or frost. The spider makes the web between twigs or other supports, and spins sticky threads around in a circle. When a flying insect bumps into the sticky threads, it is trapped. The spider in the middle of the web feels the vibrations and rushes out. It paralyses the prey with its poison fangs, and then takes the insect back to the centre of the web to eat it.

An orb web spider spinning its web

There are about **30 000** different types of spider. The comb-footed spider is no bigger than a pinhead, but some bird-eating spiders can be **25 cm** across. Some spiders live for only one year; others can live for 20 years. Tiny spiders may only lay a few eggs; larger spiders may lay as many as 2000.

## Other invertebrates

Apart from insects and spiders, there are many other kinds of invertebrate. If you spend some time in a garden, woodland or park you can find lots of invertebrates. How many can you find in this picture?

## To do: Invertebrate hunt

What to wear:

- Warm comfortable clothes – remember to wear dull colours so you don't scare the wildlife.

- A hat or hood.

- Trainers or Wellington boots.

You need to be well prepared for a field trip

## What to take:

- A notebook and pencils.

- A hand lens – thread it on some string so that you can hang it around your neck.

For a woodland, field or garden study you will need:

- A small trowel and sieve – dig up earth and sieve it to find invertebrates.

- A paintbrush – use a paintbrush to brush creatures gently onto paper or into containers so you can look at them more easily.

- A plastic spoon – gently scoop creatures up with a plastic spoon.

- String – measure around things with string or mark out an area and see how many creatures you can find.

- White margarine pot with lid or boxes lined with paper or moss – if you put your creatures in a white container you will be able to see and identify them more easily.

- A white sheet – lay a white sheet under a bush or branch. As you gently shake the bush or branch, the sheet will catch the falling creatures.

## REMEMBER

A habitat is a very fragile place and great care must be taken not to destroy or change the habitat you are investigating. Always replace logs and stones exactly as you find them. They are often homes to invertebrates. If you move slowly and quietly you will be able to discover a lot by waiting and watching. Always return your creatures to where they came from.

Here are some things you could do to study the creatures in your habitat.

1. In order to have a better look at some invertebrates that are in your garden or in woodland, you can carefully collect some soil and leaves in a jam jar. Using an old spoon gently place a few scoops into a large white shallow container. Very gently shake the container a little then, with your hand lens ready, carefully watch for movement.

   See if you can count how many different types of invertebrates you have found, and how many of each type. You can then add a few more scoops of soil, or carefully tip out your sample, and repeat the process with some more soil.

   When you have studied your sample from one area, you can try again using a sample from a different area, or from under a different log, or from an area under trees or out in the open. Make a note of the numbers of creatures that you find, and the different types of creatures. Do you have different results from your different study areas? Which habitats contain the most invertebrates? Can you describe the habitat to a friend?

   Always remember that your samples of soil are homes and hiding places for the invertebrates that you have found. You must treat your samples with great care, and return them to exactly where you found them.

2. Find out what happens when your creature meets different obstacles. Place water or stones or twigs or moss near your creature, and make notes on what you observe.

3. Make a pitfall trap. Sink a glass jar into the soil so that the top of the jar is level with the earth. Place some bait in the jar – an apple core will do – and then put some stones around the neck of the jar to hide it.

Balance a large stone on top. This will act as a roof and stop the rain getting in and drowning your creatures. Leave it overnight. Remember to check it in the morning, record what you have found, and then release your specimens.

4.    Ants leave a scent trail by rubbing their bodies along the ground. Other ants can follow the trail by smelling with their antennae. Place some food – a sugary solution in a jam jar lid will do – near an ants' nest. When the ants have found the food, move the lid of food to another place. What do the ants do? Do they go straight to the food, or do they follow the scent trail to where the food was before?

**Remember to return all the creatures to the place where you found them and wash your hands after doing these activities.**

# Exercise 2.4

Fill the gaps in these sentences, using the following words:

| six    bite    three    insects    invertebrates    eight    web |
| --- |
| two    colony |

1.    Animals without a backbone are called _____.

2.    The most common animals on Earth are _____.

3.    A large group of insects is called a _____.

4.    Insects have _____ parts to their bodies and _____ legs.
Spiders have _____ parts to their bodies and _____ legs.

5.    Spiders have a poisonous _____. This is often used to kill prey that they have caught in a _____.

# Exercise 2.5

1. What is the important difference between a vertebrate and an invertebrate?

2. What is an exoskeleton?

3. Name an animal that has an exoskeleton.

4. A snail has a protective shell. Describe how it might use its shell for protection.

5. Name the body parts of an insect.

6. What differences are there between insects and spiders?

7. Why are insects so important to farmers and gardeners?

# Exercise 2.6: Extension questions

Look at the picture of invertebrates in their habitat on page 36.

1. Make a list of all the animals you can see. Decide on a way of sorting these animals into two groups. What would you call your groups?

2. In which of your groups would a ladybird belong in?

# The honey bee and the bumble bee

Do you know the difference between the humble bumble bee and the busy honey bee?

## Honey bees

Honey bees are very sociable, and live in **colonies** that may contain many thousands of bees. Each bee does a particular job in the colony. Some bees nurse the young bees, some build and clean the hive, while others collect food.

Honey bees collect nectar and pollen from flowering plants, and use the nectar to produce honey. The pollen provides protein for the young bee **larvae** (grubs) to help them to grow. Honey bees make a large amount of honey and store this to feed them through the winter when it is too cold to fly and there are not many flowers.

The honey-bee colony has one **queen bee**, many thousands of **worker bees** and a smaller number of **drone bees**. The queen bee is the only bee able to lay eggs which hatch into new workers and drones, so all the other bees in the colony are her sons and daughters. The worker bees are all females. When they are young, they nurse the young larvae and maintain the hive. When they are older, they collect the food and guard the hive. The drone bees are all male, and their job is to mate with new queen bees.

Honey bees on honeycomb

Worker bees can sting, but their stinger has a barb, so if they do sting you, the barb will remain in your skin, and the bee will die from the injury. Honey bees will therefore only sting if their own life or the safety of the colony is in danger.

A honey-bee nest is easy to recognise because large numbers of bees will be seen arriving at and leaving the nest on warm summer days. You may also hear a low humming sound coming from the nest as the bees fan the air with their wings to keep the nest cool and evaporate water from the nectar. Most honey-bees live in man-made hives. Wild bees make nests in hollow trees.

Honey bees:
● are about 1.5–2 cm in length
● have a slightly furry thorax and smooth abdomen
● are striped, often orange and brown, or black and white
● have two pairs of wings.

## Bumble bees

Bumble bees are also sociable, but they live in much smaller groups. There may be less than 50 bees in a colony. The bumble bees in the colony will have similar jobs to those of the honey bees. They also have a queen bee, female workers and male drone bees.

Bumble bees usually make their nests in the ground, using holes and tunnels dug by mice. They build the nest from wax made by the queen bee and the workers. In the nest, they can store small quantities of honey and raise the young larvae.

Bumble bees are more able to collect pollen and nectar in cool conditions than honey bees so their store of honey is usually quite small. The bumble bees do not stay in the colony during the winter. In the autumn, the colony will raise several new queen bees. The queens will mate and then fly off to find a safe place to shelter over the winter, while the rest of the colony die out. In the spring, the new queens will search for a nesting site and start their own new colony.

The queen bee and the worker bees can sting but will only do so if they or their nest is threatened. They do not die if they use their sting.

Bumble bees:

- vary in length from 1 to 3 cm

- are fatter than honey bees

- have a furry thorax and abdomen

- are striped and can be yellow, white, orange, black or red, depending on their species

- have two pairs of wings.

Bumble bee

# Exercise 2.7

Fill the gaps in these sentences, using the words in the box below.

| drone | colonies | nectar | bumble | fatter | pollen |
| worker | pollen | mice | nectar | | |

1. Honey bees live in groups called _____.

2. They collect _____ and _____ from flowers.

3. They make honey from the _____ and feed the _____ to their young.

4. The _____ bees are all male and the _____ bees are all female.

5. _____ bees live in smaller groups than honey bees and make their nests in holes or tunnels dug by _____.

6. Bumble bees are _____ than honey bees.

. . . . . . . . . . . . . . . . . . . . . . . . . . . . . . . . . . . . . . . . . . . . . . .

# Exercise 2.8

1. Honey bees collect pollen from flowers. Explain why the pollen is important.

2. Why do honey bees make a big store of honey?

3. In each colony there are three different types of bee. Name these three types.

4. Describe the different jobs that the different bees carry out.

5. Describe how honey bees keep their hive cool in summer.

6. Where would you expect to find the nest of a bumble bee?

7. Describe the differences between honey bee nests and bumble bee nests.

8. Why do bumble bees make smaller stores of honey than the honey bees?

9. Why will honey bees try not to use their stings?

. . . . . . . . . . . . . . . . . . . . . . . . . . . . . . . . . . . . . . . . . . . . . . .

# Exercise 2.9: Extension question

If you saw a bee flying around in the garden, how could you tell whether it was a honey bee or a bumble bee?

# Chapter 3: Rocks

## Inside the Earth

The Earth was formed 4600 million years ago, when dust particles around the Sun began to join together. If you were able to slice right through the Earth you would see three layers:

- the **core** in the middle
- surrounded by the **mantle**
- with a hard outer shell called the **crust**.

**Crust**
Made from solid rock

**Mantle**
Made from rock.
Nearest the surface is
molten (liquid) rock
called magma

**Core**
Made of metals such as
iron and nickel. It is
solid in the middle and
molten (liquid) around
the outside

The structure of the Earth

The crust is a very thin layer of cool, solid rock, made up of lots of separate pieces called **plates**. These fit together like the pieces of an enormous jigsaw puzzle. They move around, floating on the hot liquid rock (**magma**) beneath.

There are two different types of crust:

- thick **continental crust** (20–65 km thick) made of **granite**. This makes up the land.
- much thinner **oceanic crust** (5–10 km thick) made of rock called **basalt**. This makes up the ocean floor.

The plates move very slowly, only about 2–5 cm each year. However, over millions of years, continents can drift enormous distances, so the map of the world as we know it today will look very different in another 100 million years.

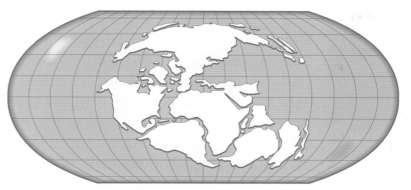

Can you see where some of today's continents were 225 million years ago?

**The Earth's surface about 225 million years ago**

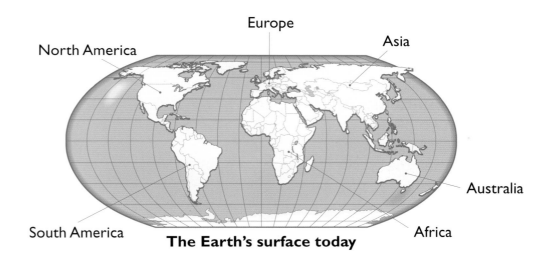

Europe

North America

Asia

Australia

South America

**The Earth's surface today**

Africa

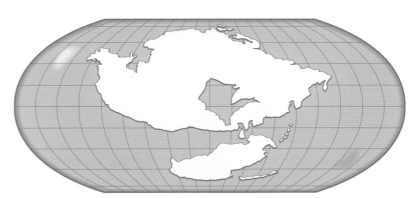

Can you see where the continents may end up in another 250 million years?

**How the Earth's surface might look in 250 million years' time**

A home destroyed by the earthquake which struck India and Pakistan in 2005

# Earthquakes

When two plates slide past each other and their jagged edges become stuck, it may cause an **earthquake**. Pressure builds up until one plate finally gives way, and there is a sudden movement, which makes the whole earth shake. The vibrations caused by the earthquake are called **seismic waves**. The scale for measuring the strength of earthquakes is called the **Richter Scale**.

# Mountains

Many of the world's highest mountains are **fold mountains**. They are made when two plates push against each other. As the two plates come together, the layers of rock become crinkled up. The Himalayas, Andes and Alps are all chains of fold mountains. Some mountains are still growing (slowly) in this way. For example, Mount Everest gets about 6 cm higher each year.

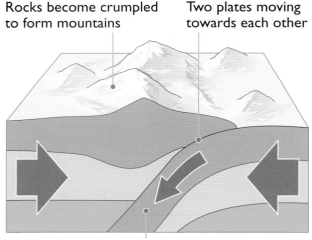

Rocks become crumpled to form mountains

Two plates moving towards each other

One plate slides underneath the other

As two plates push together the rocks are pushed up into mountains

# Volcanoes

There are about 600 volcanoes in the world. Most are found at places where plates meet.

A volcano is a mountain that is made when red-hot **magma** from the mantle escapes up through an opening, called a **vent**. The pressure builds up below the crust, and **lava** (a mixture of magma and solid rock) pushes up the vent and the volcano erupts. If the lava is very thick it may become solid inside the vent, making a plug. As the pressure below builds up, finally the plug will be blasted high into the air causing a huge explosion. If the lava is thinner, the explosion will be more gentle.

An erupting volcano

Each time a volcano erupts, the lava on the surface of the volcano cools and sets as a solid layer of rock. As the layers build up, the volcano grows larger. Where the lava is thick, it only flows a short way before cooling and setting, which makes a volcano with steep sides, called a **cone volcano**. Where the lava is thin, it flows further before setting, which makes a volcano with gently sloping sides, called a **shield volcano**.

Many volcanoes are under the sea. Some grow so large that they emerge above sea level as new islands. Iceland is a volcanic island and is still growing with each new eruption.

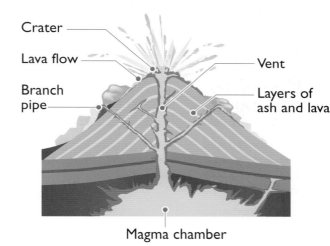

Crater — Lava flow — Vent — Branch pipe — Layers of ash and lava — Magma chamber

A volcano is made up of layers of cooled lava

## How does a rock island become a living habitat?

Young volcanic rocks on the island of Fernandina in the Galapagos Islands

Most new islands are volcanic islands. Once the volcano has stopped erupting, the island is just a lump of bare rock with nothing living on it. Islands such as the Galapagos and the Hawaiian Islands were formed in this way.

Gradually, the wind, rain and the waves of the ocean wear away the surface of the rock and break it up into little particles. This process is called **erosion**.

Animals that live or feed in the sea, such as sea birds and seals, then come on to the land to breed and their droppings mix with the rock particles to form soil. Once there is soil on the land, plants can grow. Seeds carried by wind, water or birds, are dropped on the soil and begin to grow.

When plants start to grow, it is possible for land animals to live on the island. In order to survive, the animals must not only find food, but also a place to shelter and a safe place to breed and raise their young.

Animals that can fly across water, such as birds, bats and insects, are the first animals to start living on the new island

Marine iguanas live on the bare rocks on Fernandina in the Galapagos Islands

## To do: Make your own volcanic eruption

- By making your own model of a volcano, you can see how a volcano changes its size and shape as lava flows down the sides.

- Put some play dough on a tray and make it into an interesting mountain shape. You will get the best results if you shape your mountain carefully and form ridges and valleys, and make small places where lakes might form and streams might flow. Make a small hollow at the top of your mountain, no more than 2 cm deep.

- Place some bicarbonate of soda into the hollow at the top of your volcano and carefully pour in some vinegar. The mixture will fizz and bubble. Watch where the bubbles flow like lava. Now take a small piece of coloured play dough and place it over the areas where the lava has flowed, building up that part of your mountain.

- Do this several times, using different coloured play dough each time. Your volcano should now look quite different. You can see how a volcano changes in shape and size as eruptions take place over the years.

- Now you can be a geologist and study your volcano. (**Geologists** study the layers of rocks on real volcanoes and mountains to discover how old they are and how they were formed.) Take a plastic straw (a fat, pale-coloured one is best), and gently push it down through the layers of coloured play dough and into your volcano. Carefully pull out the straw, and you should be able to see the different coloured layers of 'rock'. Gently squeeze the straw with your fingers to push out the layers of 'rock'. See how many different layers you can extract from the volcano, by drilling in different places.

Remember this is a model, and not how a real volcano is formed. A real volcano erupts when hot gases and lava explode as a result of pressure building up under the Earth's crust.

# Exercise 3.1

Fill the gaps in these sentences, using the following words:

| | | | | | |
|---|---|---|---|---|---|
| plates | vent | magma | crust | mountains | island |

1.  The hard, rocky surface of the Earth is called the _____. It is made up from lots of separate pieces called _____ .

2.  When two plates push against each other the rock is pushed up to make _____.

3.  A volcano is formed when _____ escapes through a _____.

4.  When a volcano is under the sea it may grow above the water to make an _____.

· · · · · · · · · · · · · · · · · · · · · · · · · · · · · · · · · · · · · · ·

# Different types of rocks

We can group rocks together into three groups, according to how they have been formed.

## Igneous rocks

Rocks that are formed from magma are called **igneous** rocks, or rocks of fire. As the hot magma cools, **crystals** form in the rock. You can usually identify igneous rocks by their mottled appearance. They are also very hard.

Sometimes, the hot magma under the ground cools and sets slowly, forming rocks with large crystals in them. The most common rock of this type is called **granite**. **Basalt** is also an igneous rock. This forms after lava flows down the outside of the volcano, cools quickly and hardens on the surface. The crystals in basalt are often so small that you can hardly see them.

## Sedimentary rocks

Sedimentary rocks, or **layered rocks**, are formed from **sediments**, which are tiny fragments of rock, sand, mud and parts of animals and plants. These are all washed down from the mountains by rivers and settle on the seabed.

As the layers build up, the lower layers of sediment are squashed and squeezed by the layers on top of them and slowly change into solid rock. Eventually, the rock is pushed up above the surface of the water as new land. Sedimentary rocks are not as hard as igneous or **metamorphic** rocks.

**Chalk** is a soft, white sedimentary rock that is made from the shells of tiny sea creatures. You can often find fossil shells in **limestone**, which is also made up from the remains of sea creatures mixed with some mud or clay. **Shale** is hardened mud or clay and **sandstone** is made from grains of sand squashed tightly together.

Rivers carry rock, sand and mud down to the sea

The rocks, sand and mud form layers on the bottom of the sea

The layers are squeezed as more material builds up on top of them. They harden to form rock

Layers of sediment build up on the seabed at the mouth of a river

This house is made from limestone, which is a sedimentary rock

## Metamorphic rocks

The third group of rocks are called metamorphic rocks, or **changed rocks**. These rocks are formed from other rocks that have been changed by heat or pressure. Metamorphic rocks are usually very hard.

Slate makes a good waterproof roof

**Marble** is a beautiful rock formed from chalk or limestone. It can be used for making statues and in buildings. **Slate** is layered and formed from shale. Slate is used on the roofs of houses because it is so strong and waterproof.

### To do: Make sedimentary rock cakes

Remember to wash your hands before and after this activity.

- You can use three different coloured biscuits, to represent three different layers of rock; some melted butter with a little drop of syrup, to represent sticky mud; and a few raisins, to represent dead dinosaurs.

- Put each biscuit in its own small bowl and then crush it to make 'biscuit sand'. Stir a small teaspoon of 'sticky mud' into each bowl.

- Put a layer of one of your 'biscuit sand' mixtures into a small paper cake case and press it down firmly with the back of a spoon. Place a raisin on the surface to represent a dead dinosaur.

- Add a layer of your next 'biscuit sand' mixture, add another 'dead dinosaur' raisin, and finish with a final layer of 'biscuit sand' mixture. Press it all down firmly and leave it to cool.

- Carefully peel away the paper case to see the different layers in your sedimentary rock cake.

- Now you can eat your rock cake. Can you find the fossilised remains of your dinosaurs hidden in the layers of rock?

# Exercise 3.2

Fill the gaps in these sentences, using the following words:

| igneous   animals   crystals   sedimentary   sand   metamorphic |

1.  Rocks that are formed when a volcano erupts are called _____ rocks. These rocks contain _____ and have a mottled appearance.

2.  The layers of _____ rocks are made up of very small pieces of rock, _____, mud and parts of _____ and plants.

3.  Rocks, such as marble, that have been changed by heat and pressure are called _____ rocks.

. . . . . . . . . . . . . . . . . . . . . . . . . . . . . . . . . . . . . . . . . . . . .

# Exercise 3.3

1.  Describe how igneous rocks (rocks of fire) are formed, and suggest why they have this name.

2.  Describe how sedimentary rocks are formed.

3.  Marble is a very hard rock. What type of rock is it and what was it made from?

4.  Here is a list of some of the rock types mentioned in this chapter.

| chalk   basalt   sandstone   slate   granite   shale marble   limestone |

Copy the table below and then use the information in the chapter to write the rock names in the correct columns in the table.

| Igneous rocks | Sedimentary rocks | Metamorphic rocks |
|---|---|---|
|  |  |  |
|  |  |  |
|  |  |  |
|  |  |  |

**To do: A rock survey**

Look around your home or school and see how many different types of rocks you can find. Remember to look at buildings, walls, pavements, garden statues and gravestones. You could try to find out where some of the rocks came from. They may be local or they may have come from a long way away.

# Exercise 3.4: Extension questions

1.  Copy the table below into your book. Complete the table with information about each rock type. The first one is done for you.

| Rock name | Is it hard? | Does it have crystals in it? | If it has crystals are they big ones? | Is it made from tiny shells? | Is it made from sand? | Does it have layers? |
|---|---|---|---|---|---|---|
| granite | yes | yes | yes | no | no | no |
| chalk | | | | | | |
| sandstone | | | | | | |
| basalt | | | | | | |
| marble | | | | | | |
| shale | | | | | | |
| slate | | | | | | |

2. Here is a key that could be used to identify rocks. Four of the rock names have been missed out. Use the information in the chapter to help you to identify the rocks A, B, C and D.

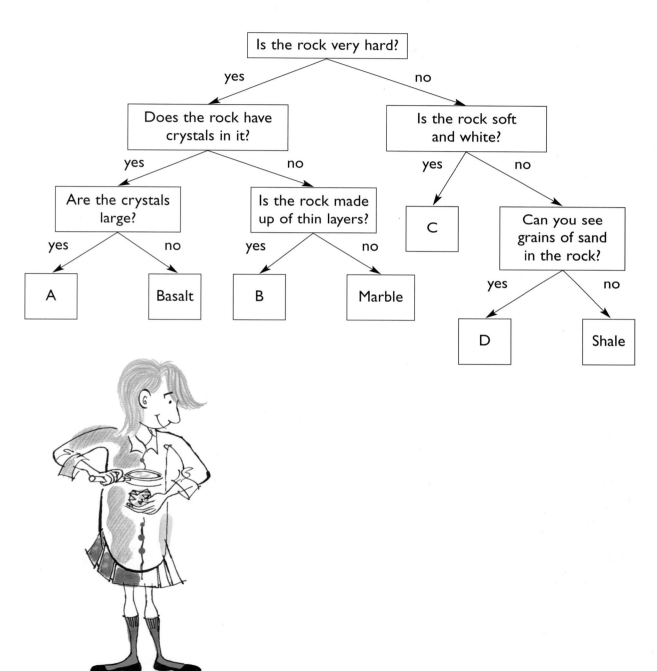

# What are fossils?

**Fossils** are the preserved shapes of plants and animals that lived and died millions of years ago and can be found in many kinds of sedimentary rock.

## The formation of an ammonite fossil

Any creature can be fossilised, providing that the body is buried quickly in mud or sand, before it rots away or breaks up.

A fossil is formed when layers of sediment settle on top of dead plants and animals lying on the sea floor or in very muddy ground.

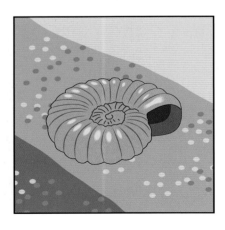

More and more layers build up. The layers are squashed and squeezed. After millions of years they harden and form sedimentary rock.

The remains of the dead animal or plant rot away and the space left behind fills with minerals. These harden to make a stony shape of the animal or plant in the rock.

Georges Cuvier (1769–1832) was a French scientist who studied the skeletons and bones of animals. When he studied fossils, he used his skill to work out exactly what animals must have looked like even when only a few fossilized bones remained. He studied reptiles and mammals that belonged to species that had been **extinct** for millions of years. The study of fossils is called **palaeontology**.

Trilobites lived on the sea floor

Fossils can give us a wonderful idea of what life on Earth was like many millions of years ago. However, it can only be part of the picture because only a very small part of life on Earth has been preserved as fossils. The most common types of fossil are the remains of small invertebrates with shells. They lived on the seabed so they were most likely to be buried quickly.

Fossils of soft-bodied animals and land-living animals are much more rare. The fossil remains that are found are usually only parts of the animal, such as a shell or some of the bones. These are the only clues for the palaeontologist, who must try to put the pieces together like a jigsaw and work out what the creature was like. Even then, it is often not possible to know exact details, for example, what colour the animal was, or if it had fur. Some fossil footprints have been found. These can help to give an idea of how large some animals must have been and how they might have lived and moved.

Sometimes geologists even find fossil faeces (droppings). These are called **coprolites** and can be used to tell us something about what the animal had been eating.

About 300 million years ago, the Earth was covered in swampy forests full of giant trees and ferns. As the plants died, they fell on to the ground and were soon covered in mud. Gradually, over many years, the mud hardened and turned into rock.

These fossil footprints show that a large dinosaur walked here about 170 million years ago

Over millions of years, the rock was squashed and heated and eventually turned into a rock that we call **coal**. If you look carefully at a lump of coal, you may be able to see the shapes of the plants that grew in the swamps that covered the Earth many millions of years ago.

## To do: Make a model fossil

- Shape some modelling clay in your hand until it is smooth and round and shaped like a bread roll.

- Press the textured side of a seashell firmly into the clay and then carefully remove it. It should have left a clear imprint in the clay.

- Press a strip of card into the clay to make a wall around the shell shape. Make sure there are no gaps. Fix the overlapping ends of card together with a paper clip.

- Your teacher will give you some plaster of Paris mixture. Pour the mixture carefully over the shape left by your shell. The card wall should stop the mixture from escaping.

- Leave the mould to set for a few days. The plaster of Paris needs to dry out and harden.

- When your model is hard, carefully peel away the card wall and the modelling clay. You can paint your model if you wish or cover it with clear varnish.

# Exercise 3.5

Fill the gaps in these sentences, using the following words:

> details    clues    coal    mud    bones    sand
> palaeontologists    shells    animal

1. To become a fossil, a plant or _____ must be covered in _____ or _____ before it falls apart or rots.

2. The most common fossils are the _____ of invertebrates or the _____ of vertebrates.

3. _____ use fossils as _____ to find out what creatures were like, but they cannot always know all the _____.

4. Fossils of plants can often be found inside lumps of _____.

# Exercise 3.6

1. What is the name given to a person who studies fossils?

2. In what sort of rock are you most likely to find fossils?

3. How are fossils formed?

4. What sort of animals are we most likely to find as fossils? Explain why this is.

5. In which type of rock might you expect to find fossilized plants?

6. Describe the sort of place where these plants were growing.

# Exercise 3.7: Extension question

Look at the photograph of dinosaur tracks on page 57. What do you think the ground was like in this place when the dinosaur walked across it? Explain your answer.

# Dinosaurs

Of all the creatures that we have found out about from fossils, the best known and most popular must be the **dinosaurs**. Stories have been told and films made about them and they are strange and exciting. But what do we really know about these ancient creatures?

*Tyrannosaurus rex* skeleton

## Dinosaur names

Dinosaurs have wonderful names, some of which are very hard to pronounce. All these strange names come from Ancient Greek and tell us something about the animal if you can translate them. The word dinosaur means '**terrible lizard**'. The name **Tyrannosaurus** means 'tyrant lizard' and **Triceratops** means 'three-horned face'. **Oviraptor** is an 'egg thief' and the name **Stegosaurus** means 'roof lizard'. **Dromaeosaurus** is the 'running lizard' and **Composgnathus** has a 'pretty jaw'.

**Did you know?**
Dinosaurs laid eggs in nests. Some fossil nests have been found and the fossil eggs have fossil baby dinosaurs in them.

## Giant lizards

Dinosaurs were members of the group of animals called the **reptiles**. They were probably not so different from their modern cousins, just a lot bigger. The modern crocodile is very similar to its ancestors who lived alongside the true dinosaurs. Hundreds of different types of dinosaur have already been discovered and geologists are still finding more and more.

When people draw pictures or make models of dinosaurs, they have to guess what they really looked like. Often geologists do not even have a complete skeleton to work from, just a few bones. They have to do some clever detective work to find other similar animals so that they can work out what the dinosaur might have looked like.

No one has ever seen a live dinosaur and so we do not know what colour they were. Occasionally, fossil dinosaur bones are found with traces of pattern in the rocks that show us what their skin surface might have been like. We can assume that they might have been a bit like modern animals such as lizards, tortoises, snakes and birds, but otherwise we have to guess. Different artists can have very different ideas about the same animal.

One artist's idea of what *Velociraptor* might have looked like

## Ancient animals

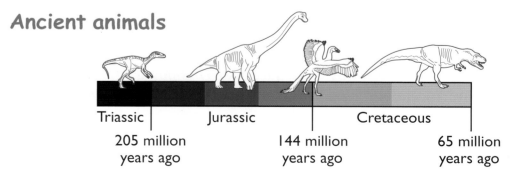

| Triassic | Jurassic | Cretaceous |
| --- | --- | --- |
| 205 million years ago | 144 million years ago | 65 million years ago |

Not all dinosaurs lived at the same time. This time line shows the dinosaurs that lived during the different ages

## Triassic

The dinosaurs lived a very, very long time ago. The earliest dinosaurs appeared about 227 million years ago in a period of time that geologists call the Triassic. These animals were mostly small and carnivorous, like the **Eoraptor** ('early plunderer').

## Jurassic

In the next period, known as the Jurassic (205–144 million years ago), the larger dinosaurs began to appear. Some huge, long-necked animals like **Volcanodon** ('volcano tooth') and its better-known relative the **Brachiosaurus** ('arm lizard') roamed the Earth, probably eating leaves from tall plants in the same way as the giraffe does today. At about 30 metres, *Brachiosaurus* was much taller than a giraffe, which only grows to about 6 metres.

**Allosaurus** ('other lizard') looked a bit like *Tyrannosaurus*. It was about 5 metres tall and 12 metres from head to tail. Not all the Jurassic dinosaurs were big. There were plenty of little animals too. For example the *Composgnathus* was only about a metre long and 65 cm tall, about the same as a medium-sized dog.

In 1861, some geologists in Germany made an exciting discovery in some Jurassic rocks. They found a set of fossil bones that looked a bit like *Composgnathus*, but smaller. This dinosaur had a beak, lots of teeth and a bony tail, just like many other dinosaurs of the period. In the rocks around the fossil bones, however, there were clear marks showing that this dinosaur had feathers. This was **Archaeopteryx** ('ancient wing') and scientists believe that this discovery proves that modern birds are relatives of the ancient dinosaurs. There are very few of these fossils; one is in London.

## Cretaceous

The next period in the geological timeline is called the Cretaceous. This is the time when many of the famous dinosaurs, like *Tyrannosaurus*, **Iguanadon** ('iguana tooth') and *Triceratops* lived. It was also the time when flowering plants and insects first appeared on land. Small mammals had also appeared at the end of the Jurassic, so at this time there were many different types of animal and plant on the Earth.

### The end of the dinosaurs

Suddenly, about 65 million years ago, it all came to an end. No dinosaur fossils have been found that are less than 65 million years old and many other species also died out at this point. What had happened remained a mystery until two geologists, Luis and Walter Alvarez, found out that a huge asteroid hit the Earth at this time. It was about 10 km across and the impact would have started firestorms and earthquakes. It would also have darkened the sky with dust, making it very hard for plants to survive. Most scientists now believe that this is what caused the dinosaurs to become extinct.

## To do: Dinosaur detective

1. Use books and the internet to find out about some more dinosaurs. There are lots that you have probably never heard of. Try to find out about when they lived, how big they were and what they ate.

2. Find out what some more of the dinosaur names mean and then challenge your friends to match each name to a picture of the dinosaur. (Here are some to start you off: *Megalosaurus*, *Giraffatitan*, *Gallimimus*, *Styracosaurus*.)

3. Use modelling clay to make some model dinosaurs. You could make up a 'new' type of dinosaur. Give it a dinosaur name to describe it.

4. Imagine a small, plant-eating dinosaur living 65 million years ago. Think about what life might have been like. How would that have changed when the asteroid struck the Earth? You could discuss this with your group and write a story or draw a picture to show your ideas.

# Exercise 3.8

Fill the gaps in these sentences, using the following words:

| colour | Greek | asteroid | Cretaceous | millions |
|--------|-------|----------|------------|----------|
| *Triceratops* | lizard | Triassic | | |

1.  The word 'dinosaur' means 'terrible _____' in Ancient _____.

2.  Dinosaurs lived _____ of years ago.

3.  The name _____ means 'three-horned face'.

4.  Fossils cannot tell us what _____ dinosaurs were.

5.  The first dinosaurs appeared in the _____ period.

6.  The first flowering plants and insects appeared during the _____ period.

7.  Scientists believe that the dinosaurs may have all died out when a huge _____ hit the Earth about 65 million years ago.

· · · · · · · · · · · · · · · · · · · · · · · · · · · · · · · · · · · ·

# Exercise 3.9

1.  What does the word 'dinosaur' mean?

2.  To which group of animals do the dinosaurs belong?

3.  Which dinosaur has a name that means 'tyrant lizard'?

4.  Which parts of the dinosaurs' bodies are most often found in the rocks?

5.  How can geologists tell what the skin covering of dinosaurs might have been like?

6.  Why was the discovery of *Archaeopteryx* so exciting?

7.  In which geological period did *Triceratops* live?

8.  When did the first mammals appear on earth?

9. When did the dinosaurs become extinct?

10. What is thought to have caused the extinction of the dinosaurs?

. . . . . . . . . . . . . . . . . . . . . . . . . . . . . . . . . . . . . . . . . . . . .

## Exercise 3.10: Extension question

In the film *Jurassic Park,* the park is filled with dinosaurs, such as *Brachiosaurus, Velociraptor, Stegosaurus* and *Tyrannosaurus rex.* Explain why *Jurassic Park* is not a good name for a place containing all these dinosaurs.

# Chapter 4: Magnets

## Magnetic or non-magnetic?

You have probably had a chance to play with **magnets** and find out what they can do. Maybe you have a toy or construction set that uses magnets to stick things together.

These children have some magnets and they are discussing what they think their magnets will stick to.

Who do you think is right?

# Attracting and repelling

You have found that some objects 'stick' to a magnet and some do not. If an object sticks to a magnet, scientists say that it is **attracted** to the magnet.

## Magnetic force fields

An object that is attracted to a magnet is pulled towards the magnet by an invisible **force field**. If you use tiny pieces of iron, called **iron filings**, you can see this force field around the magnet. Your teacher may show you how this can be done or you may be able to look at a demonstrator like this.

Magnetic force fields are very useful. We use them for all sorts of things, such as keeping fridge doors closed, joining toy trains together and even making electricity.

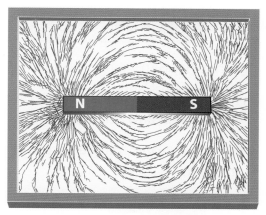

A magnetic force field demonstrator uses iron filings to show the force field around a magnet

## Magnetic poles

Once the bar magnet has stopped swinging, it will always point the same way

The ends of a **bar magnet** are called **poles**. There is a **north-seeking** pole and a **south-seeking** pole, often marked as **N** and **S**. To find out why they have these names, tie a piece of string round the middle of a bar magnet and hold it up like this.

Hold the string very still until the magnet stops swinging and then note which way the magnet points. Then turn the magnet round and hold it up again. You will find that it comes to rest pointing the same way each time. This is because the north-seeking pole always swings round to point to the Earth's north pole. The Earth is like a massive magnet and your magnet is lining itself up with the Earth's magnetic field.

## To do: Two magnets

Take two bar magnets and place them on a table, with the north-seeking pole of one magnet facing the south-seeking pole of the other and a little gap between them.

What happens when you push them a little closer together?

The two force fields are attracting each other so the magnets move towards each other and stick together.

Now turn one magnet around so that the north-seeking poles face one another.

What happens this time?

If you pick the magnets up and try to push them together, you will be able to feel the force fields pushing each other away. The magnets are **repelling** each other.

What do you think will happen if you try to push the two south-seeking poles together? Try it. Were you right?

Magnets come in all sorts of different shapes. Here is one called a **ring magnet**. The poles of this magnet are on the top and bottom of the ring.

North-seeking pole
South-seeking pole

A ring magnet

Can you explain what is happening in this picture?

We have found that two magnets repel each other if they are placed so that two **like poles** (poles of the same type) are together.

This pushing away force only happens between two magnets. An object that is not a magnet does not have a force field around it so it cannot push a magnet away.

# Exercise 4.4

Fill the gaps in these sentences, using the following words:

| south | attracted | north | repel | force field | attract |
|-------|-----------|-------|-------|-------------|---------|

1. Some objects are _____ to magnets by an invisible _____.

2. The ends of a bar magnet are called the _____ -seeking pole and the _____-seeking pole

3. The north-seeking pole of a magnet will _____ the south-seeking pole of another magnet.

4. If two north-seeking poles or two south-seeking poles come together, they will_____ each other.

. . . . . . . . . . . . . . . . . . . . . . . . . . . . . . . . . . . . . . . . . . . . . . . . . . . . . .

# Exercise 4.5

1. Each of these sentences has something wrong in it. Write each sentence into your book, changing one or two words to make it correct.

   (a) Two south-seeking poles will attract each other. ☒

   (b) A north-seeking pole will repel a south-seeking pole. ☒

   (c) If you hang a magnet up it will swing round to face east and west. ☒

   (d) Plastic is non-magnetic so it is repelled by a magnet. ☒

2. Make a list of as many things as you can think of at home or school that contain magnets.

. . . . . . . . . . . . . . . . . . . . . . . . . . . . . . . . . . . . . . . . . . . . . . . . . . . . . .

# Exercise 4.6: Extension question

Emily was given three identical-looking pieces of metal. She was told that one was made from steel, one was made from aluminium and one was a magnet. Describe how she could use another magnet to find out which was which.

# Investigating magnetic force fields

Magnetic forces can work through materials such as paper, card, wood and paint. You can show this by placing a paper clip on a piece of paper and holding a magnet underneath the paper. You should be able to move the paper clip around with the magnet.

## To do: Magnetic forces

1. Use your magnet and paper clip to find out which materials a magnetic force can pass through. You might like to start with a table, a pencil case or a book. Remember to keep your magnet away from electronic devices such as computers.

Can you explain why the magnetic force will not pass through some things?

2. How strong is the force field around your magnet? You could find out by using a thick book. Make sure that the book has numbered pages or you will have a lot of counting to do. Use your paper clip and magnet again and find out how many pages of the book you need to put between the magnet and the paper clip before the magnet can no longer hold the clip.

You could try this with several magnets.
How can you tell which one is the strongest?
You might show your results in the form
of a bar chart.

## Did you know?

Scientists can tell how many layers of paint there are on structures like steel bridges by measuring the strength of the magnetic force between a magnet and the steel under the paint. The weaker the force, the more paint there is on the bridge.

## To do: Changing force fields

We have seen that a magnet has a magnetic force field around it and that these force fields can attract or repel each other. If you have a magnetic force field demonstrator like the one shown on page 69, you can investigate what happens to the shape of the force fields when two magnets come together. You could also look at the shape of the force fields around various shapes of magnets.

# Exercise 4.7

Fill the gaps in these sentences, using the following words:

| thicker | force fields | paper | weaker | paint |

1. Magnetic forces can work through materials such as _____ and _____.

2. Some magnets have stronger _____ than others.

3. If the material between the magnet and the object it is attracting is _____, the magnetic force will become _____.

# Exercise 4.8

Here are the results of an experiment like the one on page 72.

| Magnet | Number of pages the magnet can work through |
|--------|---------------------------------------------|
| A | 92 |
| B | 128 |
| C | 57 |
| D | 293 |
| E | 41 |

1.   Which magnet was the strongest?

2.   How can you tell that this magnet was the strongest?

3.   Which magnet was the weakest?

4.   How many pages did magnet B work through?

5.   How many pages did magnet A work through?

# Exercise 4.9: Extension question

Think of another way that you could use a magnet and a paper clip to compare the strengths of magnets. Describe your method carefully. Draw a labelled diagram to go with your description.

# A short history of compasses

Compasses use magnetism to show where north is. They have been used for a very long time.

## Lodestones

Lodestones are rocks that behave like magnets. They attract objects made from iron. Lodestones were discovered a very long time ago. Over 2000 years ago, Chinese fortune-tellers used spinners made from lodestone on their fortune-telling boards.

## The first compasses

It was then discovered that these spinners always pointed in the same direction, so the first compasses were made, with a spoon-shaped pointer on a square board. The handle of the spoon always pointed south. The board had the compass points (north, south, east and west) and the major **constellations** (star patterns) marked on it.

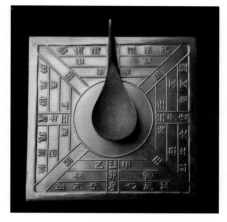

A Chinese spoon compass showing the compass points and the major constellations

About 1600 years ago, a compass with a magnetic needle inside it was developed. At first, the needle floated on water inside a jar.

A floating needle compass

Next, a box compass was made. There were two types. In some, the needle hung on a silk thread but the most useful ones had the needle supported on a shaft (small spike), like those we use today. This made it possible to use the compass to navigate (find one's way) in a boat. One of the first sailors known to have used these compasses was a Chinese explorer called Zheng Hi in the 14th century, but they were probably used a long time before that by Chinese and Arab traders.

During the time of Queen Elizabeth I, English sailors were exploring the world. One of the Queen's doctors was very interested in magnetism, especially as the compass was so important to English sailors. He carried out lots of experiments and explained how compasses worked. His name was William Gilbert.

A box compass

When iron ships were first built, sailors had problems with their compasses because the iron body of the ship affected the reading of the compass needle. A scientist called Sir George Airey, who was the **Astronomer Royal**, worked out a way of solving the problem by putting other magnets and pieces of iron round the compass in a special way.

The compasses we use today are very similar to the early Chinese ones. There are many different designs and they are a bit easier to carry around, but the way they work is exactly the same. The magnetic needle inside them lines itself up with the Earth's magnetic field and points to north and south.

## The future of compasses

Will people still be using magnetic compasses a hundred years from now? The answer is that compasses will probably still have their uses, but most people will probably use 'GPS' (Global Positioning System). This detects signals from satellites orbiting the Earth and uses them to work out exactly where you are. GPS is very accurate and even works at the north and south poles where magnetic compasses cannot be used. Maybe someone will design an even better way of helping people not to get lost. Maybe that someone will be you!

### To do: Make a floating compass

- Take a pin or needle and hold it carefully at the blunt end.

- Hold a bar magnet at the north-seeking end and use the south-seeking end to stroke the pin, starting by your fingers and drawing the magnet down towards the point each time. You will need to do this about a hundred times.

- Take a piece of card and mark a compass face on it, as shown opposite:

- Stick your magnetised pin onto the card, making sure that the pin lies along the N–S line, with the point facing towards the N.

- Carefully float your card on a bowl of still water. It should turn slowly around so that the compass lines up with the point of the pin pointing towards north.

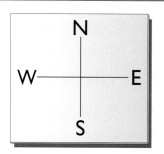

# Exercise 4.10

Fill in the gaps in the following sentences using the words in the box below.

| satellites | water | south | China | lodestone | iron | spoon |

1. A _____ is a rock that behaves like a magnet.

2. The first compasses were made in _____. They had a _____-shaped pointer and the handle always turned to face _____.

3. Early compasses had a magnetic needle that floated on _____ in a jar.

4. When ships made of _____ were first built, sailors had problems with their compasses.

5. GPS devices use signals from _____ to work out where you are.

# Exercise 4.11

1. What use was made of lodestones in China 2000 years ago?

2. What did the first compasses look like?

3. When was the first compass made with a magnetic needle?

4.  This first needle compass had its needle floating on water. What two changes were made to this design before compasses could usefully be taken onto ships?

5.  Who were probably the first people to use compasses to navigate ships?

6.  Who was William Gilbert?

7.  Why did sailors have problems when the first iron ships were built?

8.  Who solved this problem?

9.  Explain how compasses work.

. . . . . . . . . . . . . . . . . . . . . . . . . . . . . . . . . . . . . . . . .

# Exercise 4.12: Extension question

Explain why compasses cannot be used at the magnetic north and south poles of the Earth.

# Chapter 5: Light and shadows

## What is light for?

Light is a very important part of our lives. Without it we would not be able to see anything. Light can be fun, for example, when it is part of a firework display. Light can also be used to communicate.

In the 16th century, there was a fear that Britain might be invaded by the French. Many villages and towns in the south of England, especially those on or near hilltops, used a **beacon**. This was a tall pole with an iron basket on the top, which could hold a fire of burning wood. If the people spotted the French fleet, they would light a fire in their beacon to pass the message on to the next community. In this way, the message would be passed rapidly from village to village across the country. As light travels much faster than a messenger, this was the quickest way to pass information across the country in the time before telephones were invented.

Beacons were the quickest way to warn other communities of an invasion

Most importantly, without light we would not be here. Plants use light to make their food, and animals need to eat plants to survive. Without light, therefore, no animals would survive.

Can you explain why light is important to the lion?

## Where does light come from?

Most of our light comes from the **Sun** but we also get light from other things. Lamps, torches, candles, televisions and computer screens all give out light. They are all **luminous** objects. The word 'luminous' means 'giving out light'.

Sometimes things seem to give out light but they are really just reflecting (bouncing back) light that came from somewhere else. Examples of these **reflective** objects are mirrors, cat's eyes in the road and the Moon. Can you think of a way of checking whether an object is luminous or reflective? Can you think of anything that is both luminous and reflective?

These luminous objects give out light

## To do: Find out about light

1.  Look around the classroom. Make a list of all the luminous objects you can see. Then make another list of all the reflective objects you can see.

2.  Find out about lighthouses. These are a very important form of communication for people in boats, especially on dark, stormy nights. Find out how people can tell which lighthouse they can see.

3.  Communicate with light. Use a torch to send messages to your partner across the classroom. You will need to work out a simple code that you can both remember and understand before you start.

# Exercise 5.1

Fill the gaps in these sentences, using the following words:

reflective    see    luminous    communicate    food

1.  We use light to help us _____ and _____.

2.  Plants use light to help them to make their _____.

3.  _____ objects give out light.

4.  _____ objects bounce back light from elsewhere.

. . . . . . . . . . . . . . . . . . . . . . . . . . . . . . . . . . . . . . . . . . . . . . . . . . . . . . . .

# Exercise 5.2

1.  Why is light important to plants?

2.  Where does most of our light come from?

3.  What does the word 'luminous' mean?

4.  Is the moon luminous?

**5.** Below are some pictures. Look at them and then write down whether each object is luminous or reflective.

A. Star

B. Television

C. Mirror

D. Diamond ring

E. Fluorescent vest

F. Candle

G. Moon

H. Desk lamp

I. Firework

J. Compact disc

# Exercise 5.3: Extension question

Peter says, 'If the Sun stopped shining, we would starve'. Is he right? Explain your answer.

· · · · · · · · · · · · · · · · · · · · · · · · · · · · · · · · · · · · · · · ·

# Seeing

We see things with our eyes. The eyes detect rays of light coming in and send messages to our brains. The brain makes sense of these messages so that we know what we are seeing.

---

**To do: Look into my eyes**

Turn towards your partner and look at his or her eyes. What can you see? Can you name the different parts of the eye that you can see? What do you think each of these parts does to help us see clearly?

---

## Human eyes

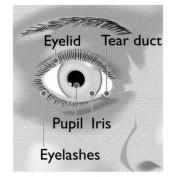

A human eye

- We can see the **eyelids**. These are like windscreen wipers. When we blink, they sweep across the eye, brushing away any little pieces of dust that have fallen on the surface of the eye. They can also close like a curtain to stop the eye from being damaged by very bright lights.

- If you look carefully in the corner of the eye nearest to the nose, you might be able to spot the **tear duct**. This allows tears that keep the surface of the eye wet and comfortable to be drained away into the nose.

- Behind the eyelids we can see the main part of the eye, often called the **eyeball**.

- At the front of the eye is the coloured part, the **iris**. What colour is your partner's iris?

- In the centre of the iris is the **pupil**. This is a hole that leads into the middle of the eyeball.

- The covering over the pupil acts like a windscreen and is called the **cornea**. This stops things from getting into the centre of the eye.

**Did you know?**
Nearly all white-skinned babies are born with blue eyes. The brown, green or grey colour develops later. African and Asian babies are usually born with brown eyes.

## To do: Close your eyes

The pupil controls how much light gets into the eye. This experiment shows how this works.

In a brightly lit room, ask your partner to close his eyes gently and then cover them with his hands to make sure that no light gets in. Count up to 100 and then ask him to take his hands away and open his eyes. Look carefully at the pupils. What do you notice? Swap over so that your partner can see what happens to your pupils. Discuss what you see. Can you explain what is happening?

We see things when light from them goes into our eyes. When it is dark and there is not much light around, the pupils open up wide to gather as much light as possible to make it easier for us to see.

Too much light can damage our eyes, so when it is bright, the pupil closes up a bit to keep some of the light out.

Inside the pupil is a **lens**, which focuses the light as it enters the eye. At the back of the eye is a layer that is sensitive to light. When light falls on this, messages are sent to the brain telling it what you can see.

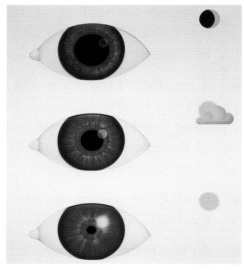

The size of the pupil changes according to the amount of light available

**Did you know?**
When the light enters your eye, the lens turns the image upside-down. Your brain has to turn it back the right way round.

## Other eyes

Vertebrate animals have eyes very similar to ours but invertebrates have very different ways of seeing the world. In fact, some invertebrates have no eyes at all. They rely on other senses to detect their surroundings.

Insects have strange eyes made up of hundreds of tiny pieces. These are called **compound eyes**. This means that an insect has a rather fuzzy view of the world.

Most spiders have eight eyes grouped together on their heads.

A fly's eye is made up of lots of little pieces

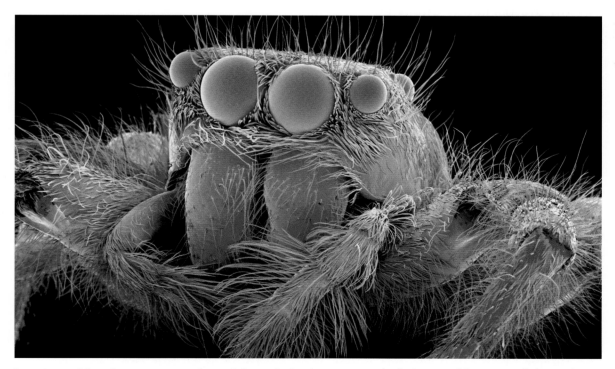

Jumping spiders have very good eyesight to help them to catch their prey. Here, six of the eight eyes are visible

Snails do not have good eyesight. Their eyes are on their eyestalks and can only really sense light and dark. The snail finds its way around by feel and smell.

The long tentacles of this garden snail have eyes at their tips

## Exercise 5.4

Fill the gaps in these sentences, using the following words:

| smaller | cornea | pupil | larger | iris |

1. The coloured part of the eye is the _____.

2. The _____ is at the centre of the iris.

3. The _____ covers the pupil.

4. In the dark, our pupils get _____.

5. In bright light, our pupils get _____.

## Exercise 5.5

1. Draw a picture of an eye and label the eyelid, the iris and the pupil.

2. What is the function (job) of the eyelids?

3. What colour are most white-skinned babies' eyes when they are born?

4. Why does the pupil change its size?

## Exercise 5.6: Extension question

Our sense of sight is very important to us. Imagine you have a friend who has always been blind. He has never seen anything at all but can hear, smell and feel the world around him. Describe an elephant to him.

# Light travelling

The light that comes from luminous objects travels through the air or space. Light travels faster than anything else. It moves at a speed of about 300 000 km per second. At that speed, it can cover huge distances very quickly. For instance, the light from the Sun, which is about 150 million kilometres from the Earth, reaches us in just 8½ minutes.

Light can only travel in straight lines. We can show that this is true with a very simple experiment.

## To do: Light detectives

- Roll a sheet of newspaper into a tube around a torch, making sure that you can still reach the switch on the torch.

- Turn on the torch and point it at a wall or screen. You may need to switch off the light in the room or draw some blinds so that you can see the light on the wall or screen.

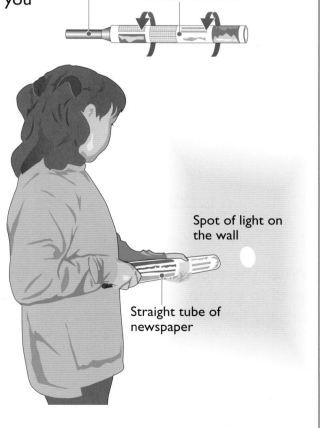

Torch    Newspaper rolled around the torch

Spot of light on the wall

Straight tube of newspaper

- Now gently curve the tube, keeping the end pointing towards the wall or screen.

- Does the light come out of the end of the tube?

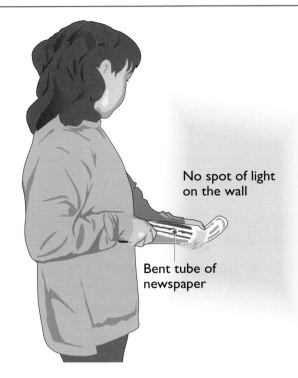

No spot of light on the wall

Bent tube of newspaper

When the tube is straight, the rays of light can pass through and out of the end.

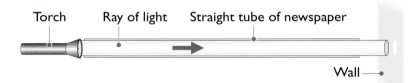

Torch   Ray of light   Straight tube of newspaper

Wall

When the tube is bent, the straight rays cannot get through. The rays cannot bend to go along the bent tube. They are blocked by the paper so we cannot see any light coming out of the end.

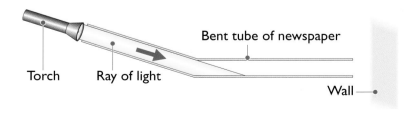

Bent tube of newspaper

Torch   Ray of light

Wall

## Seeing round corners

Because we can only see things when light from them reaches our eyes, we cannot see round corners. The light cannot bend itself round the corner to reach us. However, we can make it change direction, using a mirror. The light is reflected by the shiny surface of the mirror. If we place the mirror carefully, we can see what is going on round the corner.

### To do: Can you see me?

Make a screen between you and your partner – a large book will do. Take a mirror and see if you can work out how to hold it so that you can see your partner.

Mirrors are used beside roads to stop accidents near corners. Drivers can use the mirror to see what is coming. Mirrors are also used in some places to stop cars crashing into deer at night. The mirror reflects the light from the car's headlamps round the corner. This frightens the deer so they run away before they can be hit by the car.

The mirror can prevent a nasty accident

# Exercise 5.7

Fill the gaps in these sentences, using the following words:

| straight    mirrors    nothing    corners |

1. _____ travels faster than light.

2. Light can only travel in _____ lines.

3. _____ can be used to help us see round _____.

# Exercise 5.8

1. How fast does light travel?

2. How long does it take the light from the Sun to reach earth?

3. How can a mirror help drivers avoid accidents?

# Exercise 5.9: Extension question

A periscope is a device used to see over objects such as walls. Submarines have periscopes so that the sailors can see above the surface of the water. Here is a diagram showing the inside of a periscope. Try to explain what happens to the light from the lamp so that the girl can see it.

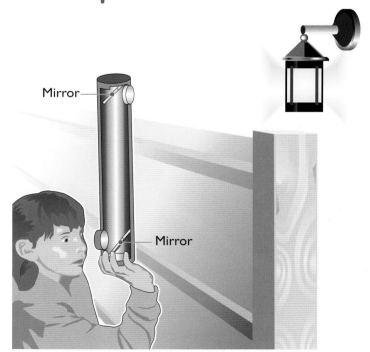

Mirror

Mirror

# Transparent, translucent and opaque

Light can pass through many materials.

Some materials, like glass, allow almost all the light to pass through so we can see clearly through them. We call these materials **transparent**.

Windows are made of glass, which is transparent

Some materials allow some of the light to pass through but scatter it or block some of it. These materials are said to be **translucent**. An example of a translucent material is the patterned glass you sometimes see in bathroom windows. These windows allow light to get into the room but people cannot see clearly through them.

Patterned glass is translucent

Many materials block light. These materials are described as **opaque**. When might these materials be useful? Do you think your bedroom curtains are opaque?

Light cannot pass through opaque materials

## To do: Draw the curtains

Little Sam in the picture on page 91 wants some new curtains in his bedroom. His mother has brought home some fabric samples for him to choose from. He likes them all but he wants to know which one would be best at keeping out the light from the street lamp.

Design an experiment to test the fabrics. You could use a torch in place of the street lamp. Think about how you will decide which one is best. Make sure that your experiment is a fair test.

## Exercise 5.10

Fill the gaps in these sentences, using the following words:

| translucent   transparent   opaque |
| --- |

1. _____ materials allow almost all the light to pass through.

2. _____ materials block or scatter some of the light.

3. _____ materials do not allow light to pass through.

## Exercise 5.11

Some children wanted to make a light-proof tent in their classroom in order to do some experiments in the dark. Their teacher found four different fabrics. The children shone a torch through the fabrics. They put more and more layers of the fabrics over the torch until they could no longer see the light coming through. Here are their results.

| Fabric | Layers needed to block the light |
| --- | --- |
| A | 4 |
| B | 3 |
| C | 5 |
| D | 2 |

1.  Copy and complete the bar chart which shows the results of the experiment.

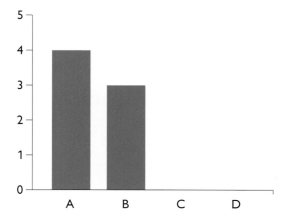

2.  Which fabric was the best at blocking the light?

3.  Which fabric let the most light through?

. . . . . . . . . . . . . . . . . . . . . . . . . . . . . . . . . . . . . . . . . . . . . . . . . . . . . . . . . . . .

# Exercise 5.12: Extension question

The children made their tent and went inside to try their experiments.
They found that it was not as dark inside as they had expected.
Suggest reasons why this might be.

. . . . . . . . . . . . . . . . . . . . . . . . . . . . . . . . . . . . . . . . . . . . . . . . . . . . . . . . . . . .

# Shadows

A **shadow** is a patch of darkness formed
when an object blocks the light.

A shadow can be larger than the
object that forms it!

## To do: Shadow puppets

- Draw a picture of a man on a piece of card. Make it simple and quite big. Give your man a face, and draw on his clothes too.

- Carefully cut your man out and stick him to a pencil with sticky tape to make your shadow puppet.

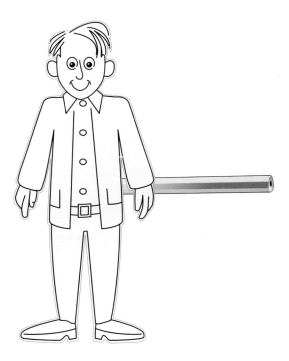

- Turn on a lamp and shine it onto a screen or wall. Hold your shadow puppet between the lamp and the screen to make a shadow. Look carefully at the shadow. Can you see your man's face on the shadow?

- Now you can experiment to find out more about shadows. Try moving your shadow puppet around. Can you make the shadow bigger and smaller? Where must you put your puppet to make the clearest shadow?

- You could make some more puppets and make up a shadow puppet play with your friends.

## Changing shadows

When you go outside on a sunny day, you can often see your shadow on the ground. Have you ever noticed that sometimes your shadow is huge and sometimes it is tiny? Why is this?

You can show how this happens by using a torch and your shadow puppet. Ask your partner to hold your shadow puppet at the edge of the table and hold the torch so that you make a shadow of your puppet on the table.

Now move the torch up and down. What do you notice about the length of the shadow? Where do you put the torch to make the shortest shadow? Where do you put it to make the longest shadow?

When you are outside, you create a shadow by blocking the light from the Sun. As the Earth spins round, the Sun appears to move across the sky. In the early morning, it is low in the sky. We call this sunrise. Shadows are very long at sunrise.

By midday, the Sun is high in the sky, almost overhead. The shadows made at midday are short. Then the Sun begins to set and the shadows get longer again.

Early morning

Midday

Late evening

The size of shadows changes according to the position of the Sun during the day

## Sundials

Look carefully at the pictures above. The length of the shadow changes. What else changes?

As the Earth spins, the Sun gets higher and lower in the sky. Its position also changes. The Sun rises in the east. It is south of us at midday and then it sets in the west. As the position of the Sun changes, so the position of the shadow changes too.

Use your torch and shadow puppet again to show this. Move the torch from side to side this time. You will see the position of the shadow move.

Before clocks were invented, people used **sundials** to tell the time. A sundial has the time marked on the base. A triangle-shaped piece, called the **gnomon**, stands in the middle. When the Sun shines on the gnomon, the shadow falls on the base to show the time. As the Sun's position changes, the shadow moves around the dial.

Sundials have long been used to tell the time

## To do: Make a human sundial

You need a sunny day for this experiment.

- Choose somebody to be the gnomon for the sundial.

- Find a clear space where there will be sunlight all day. Ask your gnomon person to stand in the centre, or slightly to the south of the space, with his or her back to the Sun. Mark where he or she is standing.

- Look at the shadow and mark the top of the shadow's head with a stick or large stone. Record the time on this marker. Make sure that no one moves these markers today.

- Every hour, ask your gnomon person to stand in exactly the same place. Each time, mark where the shadow's head is and mark the time on a new stick or stone.

- By the end of the day, you will have made a sundial. If you leave all the markers in place, you will be able to use it for the next few days to tell the time. Stand on the centre marker and look where your shadow falls.

The person's shadow indicates what time it is

# Exercise 5.13

Fill the gaps in these sentences, using the following words:

| shadow Sun gnomon short long |
|---|

1.  When an object blocks the light, a _____ is formed.

2.  Shadows are _____ in the early morning and towards the end of the day, and _____ in the middle of the day.

3.  The shadow of the _____ indicates the time on a sundial.

4.  The shadow moves as the position of the _____ moves.

. . . . . . . . . . . . . . . . . . . . . . . . . . . . . . . . . . . . . . . . . . . . .

# Exercise 5.14

1.  How is a shadow formed?

2.  Will a dark shadow be best made by a transparent, a translucent or an opaque object?

3.  Will the largest shadow be seen when an object is close to a screen or far from the screen?

4.  Which will be the clearest shadow, a large one or a small one?

5.  On a sunny day, when will your shadow be shortest?

6.  Explain why shadows get longer and shorter during the day.

7.  What name is given to a clock that shows the time by a shadow?

. . . . . . . . . . . . . . . . . . . . . . . . . . . . . . . . . . . . . . . . . . . . .

# Exercise 5.15: Extension question

Can you think of any problems with the use of a sun dial as a clock? Explain your answer clearly.

# Chapter 6: Materials

## What are materials?

What do you think of when someone uses the word '**material**'? To many people, materials are what we use to make our clothes, for example cotton, wool or polyester. To a scientist, materials are what we use to make all sorts of things.

There are lots of different types of materials. **Wood** is used to make tables and doors. **Steel** is used to make bicycles and cars. Aeroplanes and drinks cans are made from **aluminium** and lots of things are made from **plastic**. Wood, steel, aluminium and plastic are all materials.

### To do: Which material?

Take a look at these pictures. Which materials are used to make these things?

Could the objects in the pictures have been made from any other material? Work with a partner or in a group and see how many other materials could have been used.

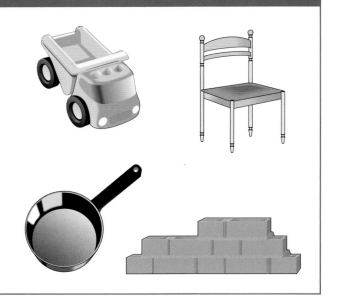

### Did you know?
Often materials can be recycled and used again. For example, some fleece fabrics are made from recycled plastic cups.

## To do: Spot the material

- Look around the room. How many different materials can you find?

- Make a list of all the materials and the things that are made from each material.

- Count how many different things are made from each material and then draw a pictogram, like the one below, to show your results.

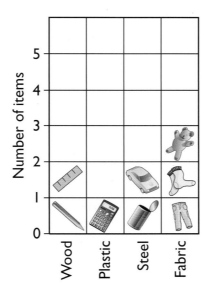

# Exercise 6.1

Fill the gaps in these sentences, using the following words:

| steel    cups    materials    wood |
| --- |

1. Objects are made from lots of different _____.

2. _____ is usually used to make furniture.

3. Most cars are made from _____.

4. Plastic can be used to make _____.

# Exercise 6.2

1.    What do scientists mean when they use the word 'material'?

2.    What material was used to make the chair you are sitting on?

3.    Suggest another material that might be used to make a chair.

# Exercise 6.3: Extension question

Here is a list of materials that you might find around the classroom. They have been sorted into two groups.

| **Group 1** |
| wood    steel    glass    brick    thick plastic |
| **Group 2** |
| cotton    thin plastic    carpet    paper |

1.    What feature of the materials do you think has been used to sort them into these two groups?

2.    Can you think of another way of sorting the same materials?

# Properties of materials

How do we decide what materials to make things from? Why is wood a good material to use when making a table? Would a wooden saucepan be a good idea?

To decide which material to choose, we need to know about how materials behave in certain conditions. A table needs to be strong and reasonably easy to make. Wood is a strong material that can be easily cut and shaped. Wood is a good material to use for making tables. However, wood also burns easily and does not allow heat to pass through it very well so it would be a silly choice for making saucepans.

The ways in which a material behaves are called its **properties**. Each material has several properties and it is important to know about all of them to make the right choice. Often, more than one property is important when making something. The material used to make a raincoat needs to be waterproof, but it also needs to be flexible and hard-wearing and to feel comfortable.

A raincoat is made of material that keeps you dry

## To do: A properties matching game

- Here are some words that are used to describe the properties of materials.

  > strong   weak   brittle   flexible   rigid   flammable   magnetic
  > non-magnetic   transparent   opaque   absorbent   translucent

- First check that you know what they all mean. Use a dictionary to look up the meanings of any that you don't know.

- Now write each word on a separate piece of paper or card. Each group will need one set of cards.

- Put all the cards on the table, face down so you cannot read them, and mix them up.

- Take it in turns to select a card, read the word on it and then find an object in the room made from a material with that property. Put the card onto the object. For example, you might choose to put 'strong' onto a bookcase because bookcases have to be strong to support the weight of all the books.

**To do: Chocolate bicycles**

Bicycles are usually made from steel. Steel is strong and hard wearing. Steel is a good choice of material for a bicycle. What would a chocolate bicycle be like? Write a story about someone who has a bicycle made from chocolate.

# Exercise 6.4

Fill the gaps in these sentences, using the following words:

| fire material properties water conditions |
|---|

1. To choose a good _____ for making something, we need to know the material's _____.

2. These tell us how the material behaves in certain _____, for example in _____ or _____.

. . . . . . . . . . . . . . . . . . . . . . . . . . . . . . . . . . . . . . . . . . . . .

# Exercise 6.5

1. What does the word 'properties' mean?

2. What properties are important when choosing a material to make a toy for a young child?

3. We usually use glass to make windows. What properties does glass have that make it a good material for this job?

4. Suggest another material that could be used in windows instead of glass.

. . . . . . . . . . . . . . . . . . . . . . . . . . . . . . . . . . . . . . . . . . . . .

# Exercise 6.6: Extension question

Buckets are usually made from plastic but in olden times they were made from metal, wood or leather. Why do people choose to use plastic now rather than these other materials? Think of as many reasons as you can.

# Testing materials

When we make an object we need to choose the best material for making it. Scientists test materials to find out about their properties.

These scientists are testing materials to see which are suitable for making swim shorts

## To do: World's strongest

When we go to the supermarket, we sometimes put our shopping into plastic carrier bags to carry it home. Sometimes the corners of boxes make holes in the bags. This can make our shopping fall out.

Make a collection of supermarket bags and test them to see which one is strongest. There are lots of ways you could do this. Make sure that you are doing a **fair test**. Perhaps different groups in your class will choose different methods. Do you all get the same answer? If not, can you explain why?

Think carefully about the best way to test the bags

## To do: The stretchiest tights

Rebecca and Alice are sisters. They both go to the same school. In the winter they wear tights. One morning, Rebecca took some tights out of her cupboard and started to put them on but they were too small. Alice put hers on but they were too big.

Rebecca thought that it would be good if tights were made of very stretchy material. Then it wouldn't matter if she had Alice's tights by mistake.

Make a collection of old tights. It is best if they do not have big holes in them for this experiment. Carry out a test to see which ones are made from the stretchiest material.

# Exercise 6.7

Fill the gaps in these sentences, using the following words:

| absorbent strong tests fair materials |

1.  Scientists use _____ to see which _____ are best for certain jobs.

2.  They could find out how _____ or how _____ a material is.

3.  It is important that the test is _____.

# Exercise 6.8

1. Some children wanted to find out which type of kitchen paper soaked up water the best. They cut a strip of each paper and stuck them onto a piece of wood.

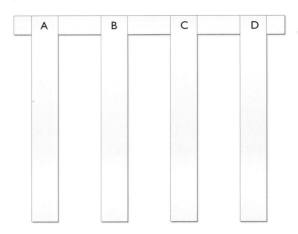

They dipped the ends of the paper into some coloured water and held them there for a few minutes. Then they took them out and looked at how far the water had risen up the paper.

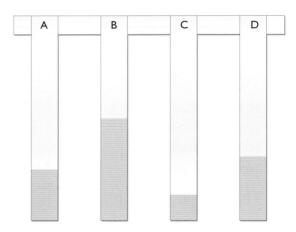

(a) Measure the height of the coloured water mark carefully on each strip of paper. Write your measurements down neatly in your book.

(b) Which paper soaked the water up the best?

(c) Which paper was least absorbent?

(d) Do you think that the children carried out a fair test? Explain your answer.

2. Many people think that we should not use plastic bags because they are not good for the environment. What other materials could be used to make a container to carry the shopping home?

# Exercise 6.9: Extension question

Paper towels need to be absorbent. It is also important that they stay quite strong when they are wet. Describe how you could carry out a test to find out which type of paper towel was the strongest when wet. Remember to explain how you would make it a fair test.

# Natural or man-made?

Many of the materials that we use can be found around us. Wood and stone are good examples. Trees grow all over the place and stone can be dug out from the ground. We call these **natural materials**.

Some natural materials must be changed in some way before they are used. **Clay** is a natural material but it is not much use in its natural state. It is soft and floppy when it is wet. It is weak and crumbly when it is dry. If we make clay very hot in a special oven called a kiln, it changes so that it becomes hard and strong. Bricks, cups and wall tiles are all made from clay.

Stone is often used for building

Bricks are made from clay that has been heated to about 1000 °C

**Glass** is not a natural material. It is made by mixing together sand, ash and limestone, and heating them up to about 1700 °C. Glass is an example of a **man-made** material. The hot glass is soft, and bottles and glasses are sometimes made by blowing a bubble into the middle of a lump of hot glass.

Glass blowing

Another important group of man-made materials is **plastics**. Plastics are usually made from oil but they can be made from other things as well. Plastics are very useful. They are light and colourful. They are waterproof. They can be easily shaped too, so they are used to make lots of things. How many things can you see around you that are made from plastic?

One problem with plastic is that it is difficult to get rid of when we have finished with it. It does not rot away in rubbish tips and it can be harmful to wildlife.

One way to deal with this problem is to **recycle** plastic objects. Another is to find ways of using plastic boxes, bottles and bags again. Other materials can be recycled too. Do you have a recycling bank near you? Maybe you have special boxes in which to collect your recycling.

The oil from which plastic is made is a natural resource and we use a lot of it. Other useful things like **petrol** are made from oil. We will run out of oil one day, maybe in your lifetime. It is important that we try not to use more of it than we need.

Some materials do not rot away so it is important that they are used again or recycled

## To do: Think about materials

1. Look at the materials that have been used to make the buildings around your school. Make a list with two columns. In one column, write all the natural materials and in the other, write the man-made materials.

2. Think about recycling in your school. Do you collect waste paper in your classrooms? Find out what other materials could be recycled and start a collection.

3. Have a recycling competition. Try to think of as many ways as possible to re-use a plastic water or soft drinks bottle. See whose idea is the most imaginative.

4. Make some plastic from milk. Skimmed milk works best. You will need an adult to help you with this.

   - Measure out 300 cm$^3$ of milk into a saucepan.

   - Warm the milk gently but do not let it boil. Next, add a

tablespoonful of vinegar and stir it until it goes lumpy.

- Pour the mixture into a sieve.

- When the mixture is cool squeeze the solid pieces together to make a ball.

- Press your plastic into a biscuit cutter to shape it and push it out gently. Leave it for a few days to harden.

# Exercise 6.10

Fill the gaps in these sentences, using the following words:

natural    useful    glass    clay    recycling
plastic    man-made

1. Materials such as wood and rock, that are found all around us, are called _____ materials.

2. Some natural materials, such as _____, need to change before they become really _____.

3. Materials such as _____, which are made by putting two or more materials together, are called _____ materials.

4. _____ is a useful man-made material.

5. Some materials will run out if we use too much of them. We can help to make them last longer by _____ them.

# Exercise 6.11

1. What is meant by the term 'natural material'?

2. Give two examples of natural materials.

3. What is meant by the term 'man-made material'?

4. Give two examples of man-made materials.

5. Which materials are needed to make glass?

6. List five things that are made from glass.

7. What is plastic usually made from?

8. Why do we need to try to avoid using too much plastic?

## Exercise 6.12: Extension question

Make an information leaflet or poster about recycling. It should be written for children of your own age and should explain why it is important to recycle materials. Include information about how to recycle or re-use materials in school and at home. Make it colourful and attractive. You could even include a quiz or competition to make it more fun.

## A lucky walk

One day in the summer of 1948, a Swiss man called George de Mestral decided to take his dog for a walk. There were lots of mountains near his home and George enjoyed walking and climbing. George and his dog walked for a long time up and down the hills. The dog ran back and forth through the grass and undergrowth as they went.

When they came home, George noticed that his dog's fur was full of little seed cases called burrs. They had come from burdock plants and were hard to remove. George, who loved inventing things, wondered how it was that the burrs held onto the dog's fur so tightly. He looked down and discovered that there were burrs stuck to his trousers too.

When he had finished grooming the dog, George took one of the burrs and looked at it with a microscope. He discovered that the burr had lots of tiny

The burrs are attached to the dog's fur

hooks on it. These hooks tangled themselves up in the dog's fur and held on tightly. He knew that this was to help the plant to spread its seeds around.

George decided that he could use this discovery to make two tapes that would hold onto each other when they were pushed together. One tape would have little tiny hooks on it and the other would have little loops. These tapes, when sewn onto clothes or other objects, would work like a zip.

He told his friends about his idea. They all laughed. They thought it was a rather silly idea but George was sure it would work. He went to visit a weaver he knew and they worked together to make the new hook and loop fasteners. They tried different materials to make the hooks and different ways of weaving the loops. At last, in 1955, they succeeded in making their new fastener work. They called it Velcro® from the French words for 'velvet' and 'hook'.

Burrs are covered with tiny hooks

Now we find Velcro® on all sorts of things. Maybe you have a jacket, a schoolbag or even shoes with Velcro® on them. It is quick and easy to use and George saw his invention in use all over the world before he died in 1990.

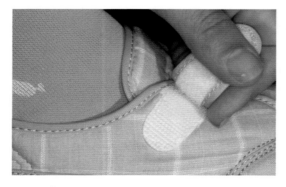

Velcro® is now used all over the world

George de Mestral was a scientist. He wanted to find out about the world around him and then used his knowledge to invent something. In this book you have begun the journey through science that might one day lead you to make a discovery or to invent something.

I wonder what it will be.

# Exercise 6.13

Fill in the gaps in the following sentences using the words in the box below.

| hooks velvet Switzerland loops burrs Velcro |
|---|

1.  George de Mestral lived in _____.

2.  George discovered seed cases called _____ stuck to his dog's fur.

3.  He saw that these seed cases stuck to the fur because they were covered in _____.

4.  He made special tapes with hooks and _____ on them to act like a zipper.

5.  He called his invention _____ from the French words for _____ and hook.

# Exercise 6.14

1.  What activities did George de Mestral enjoy in Switzerland?

2.  What plant did the seeds George de Mestral found in his dog's fur come from?

3.  How had they become attached to the fur?

4.  Explain how this might help the plant.

5.  Describe the idea that George de Mestral had after looking at these seeds.

6.  How did his friends react to his idea?

7.  Why did he call his invention Velcro?

# Exercise 6.15: Extension questions

1.  Young children often have Velcro on their shoes because it is easier to fasten than laces or buckles. Think of other places where Velcro is used and describe what might have been used if Velcro had not been invented.

2.  Any new product needs to be advertised to let people know about it and show them why they might find it useful. Imagine that you have been asked to promote George de Mestral's new invention and design an advertisement. It should be eye-catching and informative.

# Index

# Galore Park

## JUNIOR SERIES

**GALORE PARK**

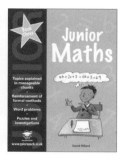

- Perfect for working towards Key Stage 2 and Common Entrance at 11+

- Suitable for the specialist or non specialist teacher or parent

- Rigorous, challenging material to stretch pupils

- Clear explanations and worked examples

- Plenty of exercises to ensure pupils have understood each topic

- Answer books also available

- Full of practical activities and interesting facts

For more information please visit our website:

# www.galorepark.co.uk

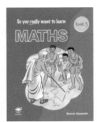